Understanding
Evidence

LONGMAN GROUP LIMITED
Longman House, Burnt Mill, Harlow, Essex CM20 2JE, England
and Associated Companies throughout the world

© Longman Group Limited 1984

First published 1984
ISBN 0 582 34115 9

Set in 10/12 pt Plantin, Linotron 202.

Printed in Hong Kong
by Sing Cheong Printing Co., Ltd.

Understanding Evidence

A resource book for sociology

P. J. North

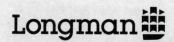

Text acknowledgements

George Allen & Unwin for an extract from *The Sociology of Industry* by S. R. Parker (1967); Associated Book Publishers for abridged extracts from *A Glasgow Gang Observed* by James Patrick (1973), *The Sociology of Educational Inequality* (1977) by William Tyler and *The Sociology of Comprehensive Schooling* (1977) by Paul Bellaby, Pub. Methuen; Basil Blackwell for extracts from *Between Two Cultures* by J. Watson (1977); Collins Publishers for an extract from *African Child* by Camara Laye (1959); Constable Publishers for an extract from *Journalists at Work* by Jeremy Tunstall (1971); the Editor, Drive and Trail Magazine for an extract from *Drive* 1974 © AA; the author, Mrs. A. Dummett for an abridged extract from *A Portrait of English Racism* Pub. Penguin; Fontana Paperbacks for an extract from *Power without Responsibility* by J. Curran & J. Seaton and *Social Mobility* by A. Heath (1981); Granada Publishing Ltd for an extract from *The Fisherman* by J. Tunstall (1967); Gallup Poll for an extract from the *Sunday Telegraph*, 22 April 1979; Guardian Newspapers Ltd for an extract from *The Guardian*, 11 May 1974; Harvard University Press for an extract from *East is a Big Bird* by Thomas Gladwin; the Controller, Her Majesty's Stationery Office for an extract from *Social Trends 1975*; Hodder & Stoughton Educational for extracts from *A Working Life* by Polly Toynbee (1971) and *The Secret Constitution* by B. Sedgemore (1980); Hutchinson Publishing Group Ltd for an extract from *One for the Money* by David Harker (1980); Inter-Action Inprint for an extract from *Football Hooliganism* by R. Ingham (1978); Michael Joseph Ltd for an extract from *Walkabout* by James Vance Marshall (1959); the author, Josephine King for an extract from 'Women's Magazines' in *Is This Your Life*? Ed. J. King & M. Stott © Women in Media 1983; National Children's Bureau for an extract from *From Birth to Seven* by R. Davie, N. Butler and H. Goldstein, Pub. Longman Group (1972); Macmillan, London and Basingstoke for an extract from *Part Time Crime* by J. Ditton (1977); Manchester University Press for extracts from *The Classic Slum* by R. Roberts (1971); the author's agent for an extract from *Coming of Age in Samoa* by Margaret Mead, Pub. Penguin (1943); Monthly Review Press for extracts from *Labour and Monopoly Capital* copyright © 1974 by Harry Braverman; New Society and the authors for extracts from the articles 'Monotony at Work' by Jason Ditton *New Soc.* (21/12/72), 'Fronts' by Ann Garvey (21/2/74), 'The Mystery of the Radical Young' by Martin Kettle (12/4/79), 'Schools for Privilege' by Joanna Mack (7/7/77), 'Busmen v. the Public' by Dr. Joel Richman (14/8/69), 'Divisions in the Workplace' by D. Wedderburn (9/4/70), 'The Tricky Games of Population Trends' by G. Weightman (16/2/78), 'Lads, Lobes and Labour' by Paul Willis (27/11/76); the editor, New Society for extracts from the articles 'Please Miss, you're supposed to stop her' by D. Hanson & M. Herrington, *Soc. Today 24* (1/6/78), 'Politics' by A. King from '*A Sociological Portrait*' ed. P. Barker pub. Penguin (1972), 'Language & Class' by Paul Medlicott, *Soc. Today 19* (21/10/78), 'Roman Nights' by T. Perry & M. Boyd, *Soc. Today* (17/2/78), 'Lies, damn Lies' by Celia Phillips, *Soc. Today 14* (29/4/77); New Statesman for the articles 'Who needs Opinion Polls' (adapted) *New Statesman* 6/2/81, 'When the Window Shopping has to Stop' by P. Kellner *New Statesman* 27/11/81 and 'The Trials of Miss Snobby Snout' *New Statesman* 7/11/80; Penguin Books Ltd for extracts from *From Communication to Curriculum* © D. Barnes 1975, (Penguin 1976), *Woman's Consciousness, Man's World* © Sheila Rowbotham 1973, (Pelican 1973), *The School that I'd like* ed. E. Blishen © Penguin Books and Contributors 1969, *So You Want to be Prime Minister* © Des Wilson 1979 pub. Peacock Books, *People Power* © Tony Gibson 1979, pub. Pelican Books, 'Changes in the Organisation of Thieving' by Mary McIntosh from *Images of Deviance* ed. S. Cohen © Penguin Books Ltd 1971, *Just Like a Girl* © Sue Sharpe 1976 (Pelican Books 1976), *Report From a Swedish Village*, Trans. Angela Gibbs © Sture Kallberg 1969, Trans. copyright © Pantheon Books 1972; Policy Studies Institute for an extract and Table from PEP Broadsheet No. 560, Vol XIII, 1976 '*The Facts of Racial Disadvantage*' by David J. Smith; the author's agent for an extract from *Soft City* by J. Raban (1974) pub. Hamish Hamilton; Martin Robertson & Co. Ltd for an extract from *The Sociology of Housework* (1974) by Anne Oakley; Routledge & Kegan Paul PLC for extracts from *The Social Psychology of Religion* by Argyle & Beit-Hallami (1975), *The Captive Wife* by H. Gavron (1968), *Bad News* Vol 1 by Glasgow University Media Group (1979), 'The Flaw in the Pluralist Heaven' by J. Bevington in *Action, Research & Community Development* by R. Lees & G. Smith, *Sociological Aspects of Crime and Delinquency* by M. Phillipson (1971), 'The Meaning of the Coronation' by Shils & Young from *Sociological Review Vol. 1* (1953), *Family & Class in a London Suburb* (1960), *Family & Kinship in East London* (1957) and *The Symmetrical Family* (1975) by M. Young & P. Wilmott; the authors' agent on behalf of M. Stacey, E. Batstone, C. Bell & A. Murcott for an extract from *Power, Resistance & Change* (Routledge & Kegan Paul 1975); University of California Press for an extract from *Behind Mud Walls* by W. & C. Wiser (1963). Whilst every effort has been made we are unable to trace the copyright holder of the article 'Holidays & Social Class' by Barrie Newman from *Leisure & Society in Britain* ed. M. A. Smith & D. Jarrie Pub. Allen Lane, 1973, the article 'The Location of West Indians in the London Housing Market' by R. Haddon from *New Atlantis* Vol. 2, 1970, an extract from *The Costs of Industrial Change* pub. Community Development Project (1977) and would appreciate any information which would enable us to do so.

To Rachel, Simon, Julian and Victoria

Introduction

Even though sociology has been taught at GCE 'O' and 'A' Level since the late 1960s there is still a shortage of effective resource material at an appropriate level. The introduction of new syllabuses and new methods of assessment means that the ability to use evidence and to analyse data is now more important than ever.

This book provides over 60 short extracts, on a range of sociological themes, drawn from many different sources: sociological, fictional, statistical and elsewhere. These extracts are accompanied by questions and issues for discussion and written work. There are enough assignments for the student to undertake one per week throughout a two-year introductory course at GCE 'O' or 'A' Level or on a comparable course. There are no chapters. Few of the extracts fit into neat categories and a comprehensive topic index is provided to enable teacher or student to find an appropriate reading. There is also a full author index which locates material from specific sources.

The development of effective understanding in sociology requires the full use of discussion and oral methods. Many of the extracts provide a useful basis for class or small group discussion. For those students who are working on their own without the benefit of tuition or class contact this collection should provide an invaluable additional resource alongside a more conventional textbook. Careful reading of the extracts and consideration of the questions could form the basis for a self-study approach.

It is hoped that this collection will prove to be valuable to all who are coming to sociology for the first time, as well as providing revision and reinforcement for those who are well into their courses.

In preparing this book I have been greatly helped by many of my colleagues at Avery Hill College, in the Associated Examining Board Social Science Working Party and within the Association for the Teaching of the Social Sciences. Yvonne Beecham, Gina Garrett, Fergus O'Sullivan, Josi Bell and Sue Procter have helped far more than they realise. Without Joan Giles' expert work in turning my scribblings into readable typescript and Marilyn Sayers' determination to get me to finish it, I doubt that this book would have ever made it into print.

Peter North
March 1982

Contents

1

Is sociology possible?

Sociology is a subject which often arouses strong feelings and arguments. Even within sociology there are debates about how sociology should be done, what it is for, even what it is about. This tradition of debate within sociology is an important part of the subject.

The extracts which follow give an idea of some of the views that have been expressed.

The main concerns of sociology may be summarised as being:

a the study of the social structure;
b the study of social composition, i.e. the nature, proportions and diversities of the various groups, categories and classes in societies;
c the constructing of accurate descriptive inventories of the social life of society;
d the study of culture and life style in society;
e the elaboration and testing of methods of research both qualitative and statistical.

These are, of course, all interconnected and in total comprise the enterprise of sociology at this point of time.

G. Duncan Mitchell *A Dictionary of Sociology* 1968

Sociology is not now and never has been any kind of objective seeking out of social truth or reality. . .

The eyes of sociologists with few but honourable (or honourable but few) exceptions have been turned downwards and their palms upwards. . .

Eyes down, to study the activities of the lower classes, of the subject population – those activities which created problems for the smooth exercise of government. . .

Sociologists stand guard in the garrison and report to its masters on the movement of the occupied populace. The more adventurous sociologists don the disguise of the people and go out to mix with the peasants in the 'field', returning with books and articles that break the protective secrecy in which a subjugated population wraps itself, and make it more accessible to manipulation and control.

The sociologist as researcher in the employ of his employers is precisely a kind of spy.

Martin Nicolaus in an address to the American Sociological Association 1968

It is not only information that people need – in this Age of Fact, information often dominates their attention and overwhelms their capacity to assimilate it. It is not only the skills of reason that they need – although their struggles to acquire these often exhaust their limited moral energy.

What they need, and what they feel they need, is the quality of mind that will help them to use information and to develop reason in order to achieve an understanding of what is going on in the world and of what may be happening within themselves. It is this quality of mind that may be called the sociological imagination.

C. Wright Mills *The Sociological Imagination* 1970

Pollner tells of a sociologist from another planet who visits Earth with a research student. The professor asks his student to carry out fieldwork on the subject of Earth societies. After a relatively short while, the student returns. But instead of his own report, he has brought with him bound copies of all of the existing sociology journals. 'There was no need', he tells his master, 'to explore any further. For there already exist these records compiled by Earthly sociologists. They tell us all that we need to know'. The professor reproves his student: 'Can't you see', he exclaims, 'that these records constitute data for analysis in the same way as do the societies themselves? For both rely on the knowledge of their members and this knowledge defines the reality in ways that we must investigate.'

David Silverman *New Direction in Sociological Theory* 1972

"That's wheat ! ! !"

2

The Coronation

Every society has certain events or celebrations which involve large numbers of people. The State Opening of Parliament, Trooping the Colour, Cup Final Day, the Boat Race, the Notting Hill Carnival, the Durham miners' gala and Remembrance Day are only a few of the ceremonial events which take place every year. In this extract two sociologists try to explain the meaning of one particular event – the Coronation of Elizabeth II in 1953.

The coronation service and the procession which followed were shared and celebrated by nearly all the people of Britain. In these events of 2 June 1953 the Queen and her people were, through radio, television and press and in festivities throughout the land, brought into a great nation-wide communion. Not only those inside the Abbey, but the people outside also participated in the sacred rite. There is no doubt about the depth of the popular enthusiasm. Only about its causes is there disagreement. Some claim that it is the product of commercially interested publicity, others that it is the child of the popular press, others simply dismiss it as hysteria or 'irrationality'. There are those who claim (with rather more justice) that the involvement in the Coronation was no more than an expression of an ever-present British love of processions, uniforms, parades and pageants. Still others see the whole affair as a national 'binge', or an opportunity for millions of people to seize the occasion for a good time. The youth and charm of the Queen and the attractiveness of her husband and children are also cited to explain the absorption of the populace.

Which of these explanations is correct? All of them, it seems to us, are at best partial answers. They all overlook the element of communion with the sacred, in which the commitment of values is reaffirmed and fortified.

Just as the coronation service in the Abbey was a religious ceremony in the conventional sense, so then the popular participation in the service throughout the country had many of the properties of a religious ritual. For one thing, it was not just an extraordinary spectacle, which people were interested in as individuals in search of enjoyment. The Coronation was throughout a collective not an individual experience.

The Coronation, much like Christmas, was a time for drawing closer the bonds of the family, for reasserting its solidarity and for re-emphasising the values of the family – generosity, loyalty, love – which are at the same time the fundamental values necessary for the well being of the larger society. When listening to the radio, looking at the television, walking the streets to look at the decorations, the unit was the family, and neither mother nor father were far away when their children sat down for cakes and ice cream at one of the thousands of street and village parties held that week. Prominent in the crowds were parents holding small children on their shoulders and carrying even smaller ones in cradles. In all towns over the country, prams were pushed great distances to bring into contact with the symbols of the great event infants who could see or appreciate little. It was as if people recognised that the most elementary unit for entry into communion with the sacred was the family, not the individual.

The solidarity of the family is often heightened at the cost of solidarity in the wider community. Not so at the Coronation. On this occasion one family was knit together with another in one great national family through identification with the monarchy. A general warmth and congeniality permeated relations even with strangers. It was the same type of atmosphere that one notices at Christmas time when, in busy streets and crowded trains, people are much more warm-hearted, sympathetic and kindly than they are on more ordinary occasions. Affection generated by the great event overflowed from the family to outside, and back again into the family. One correspondent of the *Manchester Guardian* reporting the Coronation procession, observed: 'The colonial contingents sweep by. The crowd loves them. The crowd now loves everybody.' Antagonism emerged only against people who did not seem to be joining in the great event or treating with proper respect the important social values – by failing, for example, to decorate their buildings with proper splendour. A minor example of the increase in communal unity was the police report that, contrary to their expectations, the pickpockets, usually an inevitable part of any large crowd, were entirely inactive during Coronation Day.

Edward Shils and Michael Young *The Meaning of the Coronation* 1953

1 Discuss what is meant by the following terms:
sacred rite
nationwide communion
religious ritual
collective experience
communal unity

2 What explanations have been given for the popular enthusiasm for the Coronation? Why do Edward Shils and Michael Young think that these are 'partial answers'?

3 Why do you think the writers describe the Coronation as 'a collective, not an individual experience'? What do they mean by this?

4 The writers use the idea of 'solidarity' to suggest that everyone shared in the sense of togetherness which resulted from the Coronation. Did everyone share in it, and what happened to those who didn't?

5 The sociological approach used by Edward Shils and Michael Young emphasises the idea that society is only held together because there is agreement about certain shared ideas and values. Discuss this approach in your class and attempt to work out an alternative approach that sociologists might use.

3
Walkabout

Walkabout is the story of two Australian children who survive an air crash in the outback. They meet an Aboriginal boy who helps them to survive in the harsh desert environment. On the morning of their third day in the desert Peter and the Aborigine go looking for food.

When they were out of sight Mary came down to the chain of pools. Soon she too was laughing and splashing under the waterfall. But she listened carefully for the sound of the boys' return. As soon as she heard their voices, she scrambled out of the water and quickly pulled on her dress.

The boys' arms were full: full of worworas. They were carrying at least a dozen each; and they were, Mary suddenly noticed, both of them quite naked. She picked up her brother's shorts from beside the edge of the billabong.

'Peter,' she said, 'come here.'

He came reluctantly across.

'Gee! I don't need no clothes, Mary. It's too hot.'

'Put them on,' she said.

He recognised her strict governess's voice.

A week ago he wouldn't have dreamt of arguing. But somehow he felt different here in the desert. He looked at his sister defiantly, weighing the odds of revolt.

'OK,' he said at last, 'I'll wear the shorts. But nothing else.'

A week ago the girl wouldn't have stood for conditions. But somehow, for her too, things were different now. She accepted the compromise without complaint.

They cooked the yam-like plants in the reheated ash of last night's hearth. They tasted good: sweet and pulpy: a cross between potato, artichoke, and parsnip.

During the meal Mary watched the black boy. They owed him their lives. His behaviour was impeccable. He was healthy and scrupulously clean. All this she admitted. Yet his nakedness still appalled her. She felt guilty every time she looked at him. If only he, like Peter, would wear a pair of shorts! She told herself it wasn't his fault that he was naked: told herself that he must be one of those unfortunate people one prayed for in church – 'the people who knew not Thy word': the people the missionaries still hadn't caught. Missionaries, she knew, were people who put black boys into trousers. Her father had said so – 'trousers for the boys,' he'd said, 'and shimmy-shirts for the girls'. But the missionaries, alas, evidently hadn't got round to Australia yet. Perhaps that's why it was called the lost continent. Suddenly an idea came to her. A flash of inspiration. She'd be the first Australian missionary.

Missionaries, she knew, were people who made sacrifices for others. While the boys were scattering ash from the fire, she moved to the far side of the cairn, hitched up her dress, and slipped out of her panties.

Then she walked across to the bush boy, and touched him on the shoulder.

She felt compassionate: charitable: virtuous. Like a dignitary bestowing some supremely precious gift, she handed her panties to the

15

naked Aboriginal.

He took them shyly: wonderingly: not knowing what they were for. He put the worwora down, and examined the gift more closely. His fingers explored the elastic top. Its flick-back was something he didn't understand. (Bark thread and liana vine didn't behave like this.) He stretched the elastic taut; tested it; experimented with it, was trying to unravel it when Peter came to his aid.

'Hey, don't undo 'em, darkie! Put 'em on. One foot in here, one foot in there. Then pull 'em up.'

The words were meaningless to the bush boy, but the small one's miming was clear enough. He was cautious at first: suspicious of letting himself be hobbled. Yet his instinct told him that the strangers meant him no harm; that their soft, bark-like offering was a gift, a token of gratitude. It would be impolite to refuse. Helped by Peter, he climbed carefully into the panties.

Mary sighed with relief. Decency had been restored. Her missionary zeal had been blessed with its just reward.

But Peter looked at the bush boy critically. There was something wrong: something incongruous. He couldn't spot the trouble at first. Then, quite suddenly , he saw it: the lace edge to the panties. He tried his hardest not to laugh – his sister, he knew, wouldn't approve of his laughing. He clapped a hand to his mouth; but it was no good; it had to come. Like a baby kookaburra he suddenly exploded into a shrill and unmelodious cackle. Then, giving way to uninhibited delight, he started to caper round and round the bush boy. His finger shot out.

'Look! Look! He's got lacy panties on. Sissy girl! Sissy girl! Sissy girl!'

Faster and faster he whirled his mocking fandango.

Mary was horrified. But for the bush boy, Peter's antics supplied the half-expected cue. He knew for certain now why the strange gift had been made, knew what it signified: the prelude to a jamboree, the dressing up that heralded the start of a ritual dance. The little one had started the dancing; now it was up to him to keep going. He did so with wholehearted zest.

James Vance Marshall *Walkabout* 1959

In our everyday lives we take many things for granted. Life follows a pattern which allows us to predict what we should do, how we might behave and how others might react. But this 'normal' pattern of life is not fixed, nor is it in some way 'natural' in the sense that it is part of nature. 'Normal life' only continues when everyone accepts it as 'normal'. If things change and 'normality' is questioned we must re-examine things that we have taken for granted. This may involve us in re-negotiating our relationships with others and in re-defining the meanings of things.

1 People will have different reasons for wearing clothes. They may be necessary for protection, from the cold, for example, or as a social custom. In other words, there are environmental and social reasons for wearing, or nor wearing, clothes. What kind of reasons – environmental or social – would be given by each of the characters in the story.

2 How did Mary's earlier life help her to explain:
a why the black boy wore no clothes?
b what she must do?

3 What did the black boy do with Mary's gift before Peter came to his aid?

4 Each person in this story gives a different meaning to the same object – a pair of panties. What did the gift mean to:
a Mary?
b Peter?
c the black boy?

5 Choose some everyday objects and see what they mean to different groups of people. For example, what does school uniform mean to pupils, parents and teachers, or a football club badge to another team's supporters.

'I'm a "don't know"'! "Don't know" whether to smash your face in or not.'

17

4
Talking in class

In any social situation there are expectations about how people should behave. Individuals have 'roles' to play. These roles are made up of behaviour which others expect. These expectations of the right behaviour are called 'norms'. Sociologists are interested in 'roles' and 'norms' because they play an important part in interaction. In this extract from a book by Douglas Barnes the norms relating to the roles of teacher and pupil are questioned.

Schools are places where people talk to one another. And where they write for one another. Nothing could be more obvious. But is it as straightforward as that? Isn't most of the writing done by the younger persons present? There is usually an older person called a 'teacher' present in the room where young 'pupils' are writing: does he also write? We certainly see these teachers writing with chalk on certain walls though they seem annoyed when their pupils write with chalk on other walls. What they write also seems to be rather different. The teachers also make red marks on the papers which their pupils give them. Although the children do pieces of writing to give to the teachers, we do not seem to find many teachers doing pieces of writing for the children. There seems to be some agreement about who writes where, in what way and about what subject-matter and for whose eyes. Sometimes the teacher seems to enforce the arrangement, but for the most part it is tacitly agreed. For example, we do not see any children making marks in red ink on other people's writing.

Perhaps there are also agreements about who talks to whom, and when and how. We eavesdrop on one lesson and notice that although there is only one adult in the room, she seems to be talking more than all the children together. She is the centre of everybody's attention: she asks many questions, and demands answers as of right. 'What other ways are there of measuring it?' she asks, and goes on urgently, 'Come on. More hands up. Have you all gone to sleep,?' In spite of this urgency she seems to know the answer already, for she dismisses several suggestions until one comes which she greets with, 'That's it. Good answer, John.' Her young pupils ask hardly any questions, except for permission to fetch ink from the cupboard. When one or two children shout answers without first being named by her, she checks them with a cryptic 'Hands?' which they seem to understand as a reproof. Only one child changes the subject of the conversation; he tells an anecdote about his dog, to which the teacher listens politely but with some signs of impatience. No child asks questions like those the teacher asks; no pupil says: 'What is normally awarded for an unfair charge outside the penalty area?' or continues, 'Really, Mrs Jones, I would have thought that by your age you would know something as obvious as that.'

Douglas Barnes *From Communication to Curriculum* 1976

1 What are the norms which govern the following behaviour of individuals in the roles of pupil and teacher?
a writing on walls
b making red marks on paper
c writing on paper to give to other people
d asking questions
e asking questions to which you know the answer
f shouting answers
g telling stories (anecdotes).

2 Who has the power to determine the behaviour which is suited to the classroom? How is that power exercised?

3 Choose two lessons or classes you attend and work out the roles that people play, the norms that govern the performance of those roles and the way power is exercised.

Douglas Barnes looks at the roles of 'teacher' and 'pupil'. In your class you may be able to identify other roles (e.g. bully, teacher's pet, swot, rebel, loner etc.).

5

African child

Camara Laye grew up in Guinea in West Africa. He describes the way his family lived.

At Kouroussa, I lived in my mother's hut. My brothers, who were younger, and my sisters, the eldest of whom came twelve months after me, all used to sleep in my father's mother's hut. I did not have the hut's second bed to myself. This was because the huts were so small. But I shared this bed with my father's youngest apprentices.

My father always had a lot of apprentices in his workshop; they came from far and near, often from very remote districts, mainly, I think, because he treated them so well, but above all because his skill as a craftsman was widely acknowledged; and also, I imagine, because there was always plenty of work at his forge. But these apprentices had to have somewhere to sleep.

Those who had reached manhood had their own hut. The youngest, those who, like me, were still uncircumcised, slept in my mother's hut. My father certainly thought they could have no better lodging. My mother was very kind, very correct. She also had great authority, and kept an eye on everything we did; so that her kindness was not altogether untempered by severity. But how could it have been otherwise, when there were at that time, apart from the apprentices, a dozen or so children running about the compound, children who were not good all the time, but always so full of life that they must often have sorely tried their mother's patience – and my mother was not a very patient woman.

In the morning, when, after some persuasion, we rose, we would find the breakfast all ready. My mother used to get up at dawn to prepare it. We all would squat round the great steaming platters: my parents, sisters, brothers, and the apprentices, those who shared my bed as well as those who had their own hut. There would be one dish for the men, and another for my mother and my sisters.

It would not be exactly right for me to say that my mother presided over the meal: my father was the one who did that. Nevertheless, it was my mother's presence that made itself felt first of all. Was that because she had prepared the food, because meals are mainly a woman's business? Maybe. But there was something else: my mother, by the mere fact of her presence, and even though she was not seated immediately in front of the men's dish, saw to it that everything was done according to her own set of rules: and those rules were strict.

For example, it was forbidden to cast my gaze upon guests older than myself, and I was also forbidden to talk: my whole attention had to be fixed on the food in front of me. In fact, it would have been considered most impolite to chatter at that moment. Even my younger brothers knew that this was no time to jabber: this was the moment to honour our food. Older people observed more or less the same silence. This was not the only rule: those concerning cleanliness were no less important. Finally, if there was meat on the dish, I was not allowed to help myself from the centre, but only from the part directly in front of me: my father would put more within my reach if he saw that I needed it. Any other behaviour would have been frowned upon and quickly reprimanded. In any case my own portion was always so generous that I should never have been tempted to take more than I was given.

When the meal was over, I would say, 'Thank you, father.'

The apprentices would all say, 'Thank you, master.'

Then I would bow to my mother and say, 'The meal was good, mother.'

My brothers, my sisters and the apprentices would do likewise. Then my parents would reply, 'Thank you,' to each one of them. Such was the rule. My father would certainly have been offended to see it broken, but it was my mother, with her quick temper, who rebuked any transgression. My father's mind was already on his work, and he left these prerogatives to her.

Camara Laye *African Child* 1959

Life at Kouroussa is very different from life in Britain. The climate is very different, so too are the houses and the villages. Other differences are more social. There are differences in how people behave towards each other and in what is expected of them.

1 Make a list of differences between your life and life in Kouroussa.

2 Separate your list into differences which are mainly environmental, such as different types of housing or the climate, and those which are social. You may need a third group for differences which contain both social and environmental factors.

Compare your lists with those of others in your class and, after discussion, write a short description of the main ways in which life in Britain today differs from life in Kouroussa.

3 Sociologists use concepts and theories to analyse social situations. A number of concepts could be used to analyse Kouroussa. Role, status, authority and social norms are four concepts you might use. How many different statuses can you identify in Kouroussa? What names are given to the different statuses? How are these differences shown in people's actions and behaviour?

4 Who has authority in the family? Is it possible to identify one person who is 'in authority'? Can you say who is 'in authority' in your family?

5 Social norms are rules based on what others expect of us. What are the social norms which affected these activities in Kouroussa:
a sitting down to a meal;
b helping yourself to food;
c where you sleep;
d leaving the table;
e behaviour towards guests at a meal?

6

A Glasgow gang

A Glasgow gang is not an easy subject for sociological study. It produces no documents, would be unlikely to fill in questionnaires and would probably resist any attempt to collect information about its activities. The behaviour and organisation of such a group, however, is of great interest to sociologists. To overcome the problem the social researcher needs to carry out the research without the knowledge of those who are being researched. This creates many difficulties.

James Patrick is the pseudonym of a young teacher in an approved school who spent some time with a gang led by Tim, a boy at the school. In this extract he describes the problems he faced.

I was dressed in a midnight-blue suit, with a twelve-inch middle vent, three-inch flaps over the side pockets and a light blue handkerchief with a white polka dot (to match the tie) in the top pocket. My hair, which I had allowed to grow long, was newly washed and combed into a parting just to the left of centre. My nails I had cut down as far as possible, leaving them ragged and dirty. I approached the gang of boys standing outside the pub and Tim, my contact, came forward to meet me, his cheeks red with embarrassment.

'Hello, sur, Ah never thoat ye wid come.'

Fortunately, the others had not heard the slip which almost ruined all my preparations.

D is also for Delinquent

Thanks. I'll just take the chain and don't bother to wrap it

THE SCORCHER

ffolkes

I had not planned to join a juvenile gang, I had been invited. I was a teacher at one of Scotland's approved schools. In discussion with the boys at the school the topic of gangs and gang warfare constantly cropped up. One particular conversation in the middle of July I remember well. A group of boys were lying sunbathing in the yard during their lunch hour. I was sitting on a bench among them, criticising boys who got into trouble while on leave. Tim, who had been on the edge of the group and lying face downwards on the ground, suddenly jumped up and asked me what I knew about boys on leave and how they spent their time. The honest answer was very little, nothing at all in fact. At this point the signal for the end of lunch hour was given and, as the boys put on their vests and shirts and walked over to their 'line', Tim sidled up to me and asked me to come out with him and see for myself.

At first Tim thought that I should be introduced to his mates as an approved school teacher but I soon pointed out the dangers and difficulties of that arrangement. For a start, I would then have been unlikely to see typical behaviour. It was slowly dawning on me that the best solution to the problem would be for me to become a participant observer.

I realised, however, that this method of approach presented its own problems, chief of which was to what extent I should participate. My greatest worry was that incidents might be staged for my benefit, that Tim's behaviour might be radically altered, for better or worse, by my presence. Tim's willingness to introduce me to the gang solved the problem of obtaining entreé. But from then on I would have to play it by ear. I spent the month of September thinking and planning, as the tan on my face slowly disappeared to leave me as pale as Tim and the others. I consulted no one during this period as to what my role should be, my main reasons being a need for total secrecy and a fear of being stopped. Privately I came to the conclusion that I must be a passive participant – a conclusion that became increasingly difficult to abide by. Not only had I to recognise the fact that I was bound to change what I was observing just by observing it, but I also had to contend with the problems of role confusion. The situation of my being a middle class teacher during the week and a member of a juvenile gang at the weekend produced a very real conflict for me. In fact it was the internal struggle between identification with the boys and abhorrence of their violence that finally forced me to quit.

To overcome the problem of background, I decided to present myself as Tim's 'haufer' (i.e. his best friend in the approved school), who was out on leave at the same time, and, 'havin' nae people' (i.e. relatives), had been befriended by Tim. This proved to be a simple but effective answer to questions about where I lived.

A third problem was that of language. Born and bred in Glasgow, I thought myself *au fait* with the local dialect and after two years of part-time work with these boys I considered myself reasonably familiar with their slang – another serious mistake as it turned out. So confused was I on the first night that I had to 'play daft' to avoid too many questions and also to enable me to concentrate on what was being said.

The plan was to meet Tim on the Saturday evening of his next weekend leave. Boys from Glasgow and the surrounding area were allowed home for a weekend once a month and for Sunday leave in the middle of the month. I began to concentrate on making my physical appearance acceptable to the group. I was prepared to give my age as seventeen, although this point was never questioned. In fact I was able to pass myself off as a mate of a fifteen year old boy; my exact age remained indeterminate but apparently acceptable. Clothes were another major difficulty. I was already aware of the importance attached to them by gang members in the school and so, after discussion with Tim, I bought the suit I have described in the first paragraph. Even here I made two mistakes. Firstly, I bought the suit outright with cash instead of paying it up, thus attracting both attention to myself in the shop and disbelief in the gang when I innocently mentioned the fact. Secondly, during my first night out with the gang, I fastened the middle button of my jacket as I was accustomed to do. Tim was quick to spot the mistake. The boys in the gang fastened only the top button; with this arrangement they can stand with their hands in their trouser pockets and their jackets buttoned – 'ra gallous wae'.

James Patrick *A Glasgow Gang Observed* 1973

1 What preparations did James Patrick make before he started his study? Why were these preparations necessary?

2 What problems did he have to face?

3 Why do you think James Patrick chose to spend his time with a group like this? What sociological value might such a study have?

4 Some sociologists are concerned about the moral problem of studying groups of people without their knowledge or their permission. Often the people researched are under-privileged and without power while the researcher has a good job and hopes for a bright future as a result of the research. Do you think this is a problem? What might be done to overcome it?

5 In what other situations might this form of 'covert' or 'undercover' research be used? Why?

7

The tricky game of population trends

Predicting population trends is as frustrating and amusing as long range weather forecasting. The Royal Commission, set up in 1944 to examine the unprecedented decline in births during the 1930s, reported in 1949 two years after the baby boom of 1947. Then, after 1954, the birth rate took off and ten years later reached its highest point for 50 years. Scrambling to keep pace with events, government statisticians kept revising their predictions upwards. Then, at the end of 1964, the birth rate began to fall, plummeting after 1971 into a decline which only now may just have halted.

Projected population by the end of the century has varied between 50 and 72 million, and estimated live births by the year 2000 have swung between 650,000 and 1,500,000 per annum (see Figure 9). It's easy to scoff at the tendency of demographers in the past to take a recent trend and extend it into the future. But the tricky variable is fertility – the number of babies people decide to have, and the time they decide to have them – and to know what is going to happen, you have to predict human behaviour.

Explaining past behaviour is difficult enough and amounts in the end to a collection of competing theories. All you can be sure of is the mechanics of marriages, birth rates, family size, and so on. It is quite a different exercise to say *why* people did what they did.

Up to point, we do know what 'caused' the rise in births in the decade 1954–64. A catching up on delayed childbirth by women who had postponed building their family, coincided with a younger generation of women marrying younger and having their children early. There was also a decrease in childlessness, and a slight increase in overall family size. Since 1964, there has been a coincidence of one generation of women who had completed their families early, while another generation were delaying childbirth. So babies got 'spread thin'. There has also been a decrease in three and four child families, and a general convergence of family size around two. But we don't know how large, on average, the completed family size of women married over the last few years will be. As the age of marriage has fallen (and risen again slightly), the timing and spacing of births within marriage is important in annual birth rates.

Among the many influences on the annual birth rate, like the age at marriage, or the number of women of child-bearing age in the population, the most important is the desire of people to have children. To a lesser extent, their success in not having children if they don't want them, is also important. On this latter point, there is a very common misconception about the role of family planning services and contraception in declining birth rates.

Of all the theories – economic, sociological and otherwise – of why the birth rate should have fallen since 1964, the most obvious and commonsensical – that is because of modern contraceptives – is the most easily refuted.

First, the decline in births in the 1930s was achieved without wide use of contraceptives. Secondly, the post-war decline in births in many developed countries from around the mid-1960s has been managed with patterns of contraceptive use which differ widely.

Birth rates have declined not only without the aid of effective contraceptives, but also in the face of government policies encouraging population growth. The refusal of people to respond to official exhortation is really quite heartwarming, though at what personal cost they have managed it we don't know.

Just as the absence of effective modern contraceptives does not imply a rocketing birth rate, so the greater use of them does not promise a decline. At the same time as surveys in Britain showed a more widespread adoption of modern forms of contraception, the birth rate was going up – in the 1954–64 period. So any simple formula equating, for example, the introduction of the pill here in 1962 and the decline in births from 1964 will not stand up to analysis. Nor can the legalisation of abortion in 1967 be held responsible for much of the decline. We don't know how many illegal abortions were performed before the Abortion Act was passed, but the great rise in legal – and so statistically recorded – abortions since 1968, reaching a peak of 112,000 in 1974, was still small in relation to the birth fall.

Though the availability and take-up of effective contraceptives is not a necessary condition for a fall in the birth rate, it does not follow that recent changes in birth control practice will have no effect on population trends. Ann Cartwright, who has carried out a number of family planning surveys, believes that the greater use of modern contraceptives has changed a 'whole heap of things' including women's expectations about childbirth.

Gavin Weightman *New Society* 16 February 1978

1 What have been the trends in the birth rate since 1930?

2 Why did the birth rate rise between 1954 and 1964?

3 What caused the fall in the number of births after 1964?

4 Explain why you either agree or disagree with the following statements:
a Predicting future population trends simply involves taking the present trend and continuing it into the future.
b Before you can predict future trends it is not enough just to know what people did in the past. You also need to know why they did it.
c The fall in the birth rate was caused by greater use of contraceptives and easier abortion.

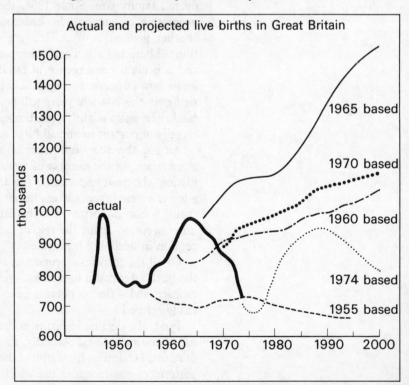

Actual and projected live births in Great Britain

8

Top of the Pops

Perhaps the best known, and most extensively read British survey is the weekly list of best selling records. Compiling the Top Forty is not an easy task.

Up to 1969, the British charts were a joke. *Melody Maker* began compiling the first one in 1947, based on wholesale orders for sheet music, not on sales figures. ('Tennessee Waltz' is reputed to be the last song to sell over a million copies as sheet music, in 1950). The *New Musical Express* (*NME*) produced the first chart (the top fourteen) based on records in 1952. For almost twenty years these charts were the standard reference inside and outside the music industry for market popularity, but their laxness and built-in inadequacies were fabled. *NME* sent out questionnaires to 250 retail shops, and usually got half of them returned. They asked not for sales figures, but for something called 'the order of customer's preference'. The scope for mistakes, not to mention deliberate distortion and manipulation, was enormous. If you wanted to push a record – if you were one of the full-time songpluggers, say – all you had to do was to discover fifty or so of the shops used by *NME*, and arrange for twenty copies of your record to be bought at each. At 1968 prices, this would have cost you around £450, and you could always recoup part of your 'investment' by selling the thousand records off cheap. Such a sale would guarantee a place at the bottom end of the chart – even in 1970, 500 singles sold in any one day could get a record into the Top 50. Once the record appeared in the chart, it inevitably attracted the attention of disc jockeys and radio producers, and the owners of other retail shops. Given that the song was any good at all, you'd improved your chances of real market success no end.

Eventually, so great was the industry distrust of the accuracy of the *NME* charts that the BBC decided to sponsor its own. From 1969, the British Market Research Bureau began producing a new chart for the Corporation and *Music Week*. They choose 300 shops, and get returns from about 75 per cent each week. But two of the largest retailers, Boot's and Smith's, refuse to cooperate. (Smith's have been Britain's largest record sellers since 1963.) So scrupulous are the BMRB that returns are vetted and cross-checked for signs of manipulation. By the time the charts are published the information they contain can be a fortnight out of date! In any case, these charts are subject to the same built-in distortions as the *NME* ones. The large difference in sales between a number 1 and a number 2 record draws attention away from the tiny differences between, say, number 30 and number 31, where the margin of error in the statistical sample could quite falsify the position of dozens of records.

Dave Harker *One for the Money* 1980

1 Why were the 1947 *Melody Maker* charts not an accurate indication of the music people were buying?

2 Describe three ways in which the *New Musical Express* charts might become distorted or manipulated?

3 What are the problems that would need to be overcome in producing a popular music chart which accurately reflect the music people like best?

4 Conduct a survey among students in your school or college of:
a their favourite records;

b the records or album they have bought within the last week. Compare your findings with those of the BMRB which are published in *Music Week*.

9

On the buses

In many social situations there is a struggle for control. Joel Richman describes how bus drivers and conductors maintain their positions and attempt to socialise the public into the role of 'good passengers'.

Though the driver is physically separated from the passengers in certain types of bus, this does not always make him feel socially immune from them. Those drivers who aim to please the passengers and who take a pride in giving a fast, smooth ride, will blast the horn viciously and dramatically throw their hands in the air when they are forced to pull up sharply because of the misdemeanours of other road users, in order to absolve themselves from blame in the eyes of their passengers. The passengers are then usually stimulated into a series of group discussions about 'madmen on the road today' and 'the things busmen have to put up with'. The driver may also use this ruse when he is at fault, because this means less criticism from passengers will fall on his conductor: in the public's eye, driver and conductor are often indistinguishable in times of trouble.

The bus, as a physical object, can be made to transmit a wide range of messages to the waiting passengers. When he is running late in 'office hours' in an area where passengers are likely to be vocal and report busmen, the good driver will try to transmit the message that he had been moving heaven and earth to arrive at all.

This he does by accelerating near the stop, then pulling up with brakes screeching loudly. If the conductor is also experienced, he will reinforce the drama by positioning himself on the platform to greet the boarding passengers with a facial expression which is a mixture of harassment and apology. However, the same performance in a different setting – as with lower working class passengers at pub closing time – will produce a different response: antagonism towards the bus crew.

As a work group, busmen have developed a loose code of ideal passenger conduct to protect their status. They don't like the public trying to undermine it. Thus, a waiting passenger should halt a bus at a stop with a modest gesture of the outstretched arm, made in 'good time'. Working class teenagers who make no arm gesture, or stick out a foot instead, are 'missed', or made to 'run for it', by the driver pulling up well past the stop. The middle class, who flag the bus down with an up and down movement of the arm, or substitute an object, especially an umbrella, even in good time, are equally resented for their unnecessary, ostentatious display of assumed authority.

Like drivers, conductors must not be forced, without justification, into an obvious, servile role. Able-bodied passengers are not helped on or off with their luggage. When a married couple have a child in a pushchair at a stop, the wife often hands the child to her husband, while she expects the conductor to help her on with the folded up trolley. This marital manoeuvre is countered by the conductor, who is usually to be found performing his duties in an efficient manner upstairs. Blatant strategies by passengers to keep the busman in his place as 'servant' are more difficult for the conductor to deal with.

For example, a passenger who slowly and methodically searches through his pockets for 'rubbish' (the busmen's word for copper), is seen as attempting to gear the conductor to his rhythm of action by keeping him hovering around. A more extreme situation is when a passenger says nothing and doesn't change his expression when the conductor comes along. Inexperienced conductors often lose their temper, but the more experienced ones leave the stage, usually saying something like: 'I'll be back when you know what you want.'

Busmen see the 'training' of their passengers into the correct attitude as an integral part of their job. The public must respond with gratitude when a 'favour' is performed. An example of this occurred when one conductor stepped on to the pavement, righted a pushchair and placed a small child in it. The anxious mother with two older children turned to move away when the conductor suddenly caught her arm and said in a loud, sarcastic voice: 'Don't forget to say thank you, will you?'

In another incident a driver had just started his new track, from a middle class suburb to the centre of town, and arrived five minutes later than the passengers were used to. In a brisk manner, some of them told him this, they dismissed the driver's explanation as irrelevant. The next day the journey was ten minutes slower. The now irate passengers (who, in their own minds, had the driver already dismissed) in delegation brought over the inspector, who examined the driver's timeboard, and then solemnly informed the passengers there was nothing either he or anyone else could do, for the bus had arrived at the correct time! It had been the regular practice of drivers to make ten minutes on this long track for a tea break at the terminus, which pleased crew and passengers alike. For the rest of the week the bus reached its destination at its scheduled time. The crew missed their brew, but enjoyed the subjection and humiliation suffered by their passengers.

Joel Richman *Busmen versus the public* 1969

1 What do you understand by the following terms?
immune
misdemeanors
ruse
'reinforce the drama'
subjection

2 How does the driver attempt to get the passengers on his side against other road users?

3 In any social situation individuals present an image of how they want others to see them. What kind of 'images' do bus conductors try to present to their passengers?

4 How does the bus crew train passengers
a to be polite?
b to give the right money?

c give the 'correct' signal at a bus stop?
d to be grateful?

5 How might a bus driver or conductor describe his or her view of an ideal passenger?

10

On the terraces

Sociologists use the term 'career' to describe the way an individual moves from stage to stage through his or her life. You can have a number of careers in different areas of your life. There is your school career, your sporting career, your career as a disco dancer or your voluntary service career. Careers are marked by the movement from one status to the next. Each status brings new ways of behaving, new things to learn and new expectations to fulfil.

Peter Marsh used this concept of career to explain events on the terraces at a football ground.

The football terraces provide an alternative career structure – an orderly framework for making progress in the society of the terrace. Unlike careers in the outside world there's no financial reward to be gained. The payoff is in social terms. But the benefits are still tangible and real. To young working class kids for whom school, work or the dole queue offer little in the way of potential for personal achievement, the availability of an alternative world in which to become somebody is attractive. And so, boys of 9, 10, or 11 are drawn to the terraces by the prospect of immediate membership of a society which offers excitement, danger and a tribal sense of belonging. These are the 'novices' or 'little kids' at the start of their apprenticeship.

'They'll go up and do all the signs and they'll chant "come on", "up the aggro" and everything like that, and then as soon as anything happens they'll run everywhere and put everything into panic and you don't know where you are.'

To older fans, 'novices' are a bit of an embarrassment because they don't really know what they are doing. Their knowledge of the codes of conduct is limited and superficial. But acquisition of appropriate knowledge and skill is made easier by the fact that there is a distinct model to which they are aspiring. The model is the 'hooligan' or, being less emotive, the 'rowdy'. 'Rowdies' are the energetic lads on the terraces. They are the ones who sing and chant the loudest, wear the most extreme forms of 'gear' and run around a lot. They are also the people magistrates describe as animals, morons and thugs.

'Rowdies' form the core membership of the terrace culture. Their average age is 15 or 16 and although there are no initiation rites or entry ceremonies – in fact any supporter can join in a superficial sense – the 'men' are separated from the 'boys' in situations which demand specific action. Only by matching up to the standards expected, and by demonstrating commitment to the commonly held values and ideals, can the 'rowdy' hope to be recognised by his peers.

'I mean it don't matter really if you lose a fight, so long as you don't back down. I mean you could end up in hospital but so long as you didn't back down you'd prove your case. I mean there's a lot of this not wanting to be called a coward in it. When you're sixteen or seventeen, before say you're courting steady and that, that's the time when you don't like being called a coward. And it's one thing that hurts you more than anything else you know.'

One very favourable role within the rowdy group is that of the fan who aspires to being an 'aggro leader' or, more colloquially, a 'hard-case'. They are the ones who will lead running charges at the opposition fans, both inside and outside the ground, and they will figure prominently in the scuffles which break out. Being a 'hard-case' gets you the best seat on coaches to away matches; 'novices' buy you beers and other fans show a satisfying deference. Such a position can be held, informally, without bullying or coercion. It does, however, require a certain degree of fearlessness.

'I think we were at Bradford City and we knew that right at the end of the match they were all going to come over the fences and over walls and everything and it were just going to be one helluva Custer's last stand. And there were about fifty or sixty who fought against something like three hundred. We never stood a chance but we knew that we couldn't really back down against them, and after we'd stood there on the hill and we'd been beaten, I mean you could see youths, Bradford supporters, carrying Chesterfield supporters out of the ground back to the buses. And you could see Chesterfield supporters carrying Bradford City supporters back to the buses, I mean after the fight. I mean, you know, that were it.'

That's how the 'hard-case' builds his reputation. Again, he does it not by causing serious injury to other people, but by consistently demonstrating a determination to stand up for himself and his group. But his fearlessness is limited. For the total absence of fear is an aspect of character more typical of the 'nutter' than the 'hard-case'.

'Well, for me somebody who's hard does not necessarily have to start the trouble or be the cause of it. Some people that are described as nutters or headbangers may not necessarily be physically hard, it's just that they've got the nerve, more than anything else, to do something that is considered out of the ordinary, and that's what they get their reputation for – not so much being hard in the one to one confrontation or something, but actually having the nerve to charge into a situation that they know they're gonna come out the losers.'

'Nutters' 'go crazy' or 'go mad' – they go beyond the fans' limits of acceptable and sane behaviour. In doing so, however, everybody else on the terraces comes to understand more clearly where those limits lie. In fact, the existence of 'nutters' is proof of the existence of order in the first place. If random action was the norm, 'nutters' would be indistinguishable from anybody else. But the fact that they are viewed, from the inside, as deviant, provides us with a very useful way of assessing the nature and extent of the informal terrace rules. We can look at what shouldn't be done, which is always an easier task than teasing out what should.

Peter Marsh *Life and careers on the football terraces* 1978

1 What do you think Peter Marsh means when he uses the following terms?

career

codes of conduct

a distinct model to which they are aspiring

terrace culture

peers

deviant

order

2 In this extract Marsh describes four different groups of supporters. Each group has a particular status within the football crowd and distinctive ways of behaving. The youngest group are the 'little kids' or 'novices'. They are an embarrassment to the older fans because they try to copy the older boys but as soon 'as anything happens they'll run everywhere and put everything into a panic'. What are the other three groups and how do they behave? How is each group viewed by the other supporters?

3 Why does Peter Marsh suggest that 'the existence of "nutters" is proof of the existence of order'.

4 In what ways is the sociologist's way of looking at football crowds different from that of the mass media, magistrates and other 'law abiding citizens'?

"We were on our way to a fancy-dress party."

11
A Roman night-out

Tina Perry and Margaret Boyd were studying sociology for GCE 'A' Level at a community college in Leicestershire. They were set the task of carrying out some participant observations on how people create impressions in social interaction. This is their report:

Situation: Adelphi Hotel charity ball in Roman fancy dress. Our role as participant observers was to be 'pretty little flower girls'. Our backstage entrance – unfortunately made through the main doors of the hotel – was somewhat unrehearsed. Flustered, due to lack of time to get ready, we arrived in jeans, curlers in the hair, with armfuls of baggage. A polite but bewildered receptionist mistook us for the song and dance act and when she discovered that we were only flower girls – she was not so helpful. Naturally, in the posh surroundings of the Adelphi, we felt a little out of place, but as soon as we acquired the necessary props – the Roman dress, hairstyle, make up, we began to feel the part and were accepted by others in our role . . . time for the dramatic entrance!

Before guests arrived, we were chatting quite normally to the president who confessed 'I wish I was at home watching the television!' but as soon as the couples arrived, she instantly took up her accepted front-stage performance: 'How lovely to see you, so glad you could come.' We quickly assumed character and the appropriate expressions – instead of 'would you like a flower?' it was on with the smile and 'would you care for a carnation?' 'Which colour would you prefer . . . the pink with your purple patterned dress? . . . lovely!' (What revolting taste, dear!) We became very aware that we were acting out a 'role' and became quite practised at our 'expressions given off'.

The organiser, Julius Caesar (alias Harry) portrayed a calm exterior in front of the other guests, but when the Lord Mayor arrived, Caesar developed an attack of 'first night nerves'. He delivered his opening speech (prepared in the bath) with the eloquence and subordination befitting a grovelling student. The Lord Mayor seemed a little taken aback by this embarrassing performance and did his best to assure the poor Emperor that – yes a Roman evening was a splendid and original idea, and yes he was sure it was going to be a big success. The Lady Mayoress, however, wasn't quite able to 'manage her impressions' as well as hubby, and was heard to remark to no one in particular 'I have to come here ever such a lot, once I had to come four times in one week' (sigh!). They were about to make an entrance into the dining hall but Harry made them wait until after a tape of a marching escort had been played!

We decided at this point to take a look 'behind the scenes' – the kitchen. The waitresses were appropriately dressed in black and white as they marched in and out with the silveware piled high with dishes from the 12-course meal. But as soon as they got back stage it was out with the fags and 'Ooh bloody 'ell, me feet are killing me' – the smart white gloves were then removed as they dunked their 'pinkies' into the oyster soup! Having previously been impressed by the stuffed olives, we discovered that they were advailable on offer at Tesco, as were the tins of *instant* coffee and the tinned fruit salad!

Waiting back-stage for their entrance were the Beverly Sisters, the star attraction who didn't appear to be too concerned by making their grand entrance through the kitchen (despite the fact that their red and pink outfits clashed horribly with the *instant* whip).

Following the cabaret came the perfect opportunity to observe the continuing saga of 'keeping up with the Jones', only in this case it was with the Ponsonby-Smythes! Our new role was to sell raffle tickets at £5 each. It was interesting to observe the increasing generosity as we moved along the 'banquet tables'. '3 for you sir? thank you . . . and you sir – 5? certainly . . . 16 sir? (80 quid!?) That's £80 sir, thank you.'

Whilst back-stage interacting (!!) with some Centurians, we indulged in a little ethnomethodological experiment – we appeared to be quite ignorant of the rather debauched implications of a seedy story, and although we were quite eager to be educated in such matters, they appeared most reluctant to explain the implications (tee hee!). We realised that this was because they were unfamiliar with out little ways; our friends who weren't involved in the observation saw through our little trick!

So ended an evening of considerable entertainment – to us at least!

Tina Perry and Margaret Boyd *Roman Nights* 1978

1 What role were the girls expected to play?

2 How did the receptionist's manner change when she realised that she had mistaken the girls' role?

3 Costumes and 'props' were used to 'create' the roles people played at the ball. How are similar 'props' used in everyday life to create roles?

4 Did the girls behave 'naturally' when handing out the flowers?

5 Who was better at 'managing impressions' – the Lord Mayor or the Mayoress?

6 How did the waitresses's behaviour in the kitchen differ from their behaviour in the dining hall.

7 Television comedy shows often exploit the contrast between how one actor wants others to believe he is, and how he really is. Write a description of such a comedy scene.

8 Carry out your own participant observation study of how people 'manage' social interactions. Possible locations might be:
– a shoe shop
– a restaurant
– a school or college staff room
– a school journey
– an interview.

12

Shooting an elephant

George Orwell was, for a number of years, a senior officer in the British Imperial Police Force stationed in Burma. One day he was called to deal with a marauding elephant that was causing damage and had trampled a native to death.

'I had halted on the road. As soon as I saw the elephant I knew with perfect certainty that I ought not to shoot him. It is a serious matter to shoot a working elephant – it is comparable to destroying a huge and costly piece of machinery – and obviously one ought not to do it if it can possibly be avoided. And at that distance, peacefully eating, the elephant looked no more dangerous than a cow. I thought then and I think now that his attack of 'must' was already passing off; in which case he would merely wander harmlessly about until the mahout (elephant driver) came back and caught him. Moreover, I did not in the least want to shoot him. I decided that I would watch him for a little while to make sure that he did not turn savage again, and then go home.

'But at that moment I glanced round at the crowd that had followed me. It was an immense crowd, two thousand at the least and growing every minute. It blocked the road for a long distance on either side. I looked at the sea of yellow faces above the garish clothes – faces all happy and excited over this bit of fun, all certain that the elephant was going to be shot. They were watching me as they would watch a conjurer about to perform a trick. They did not like me, but with the magical rifle in my hands I was momentarily worth watching. And suddenly I realised that I should shoot the elephant after all. The people expected it of me and I had got to do it; I could feel their two thousand wills pressing me forward, irresistibly. And it was at this moment, as I stood there with the rifle in my hands, that I first grasped the hollowness, the futility of the white man's dominion in the East. Here was I, the white man with his gun, standing in front of the unarmed native crowd – seemingly the leading actor of the piece; but in reality I was only an absurd puppet pushed to and fro by the will of those yellow faces behind. I perceived in this moment that when the white man turns tyrant it is his own freedom that he destroys. He becomes a sort of hollow, posing dummy, the conventionalised figure of a sahib. For it is the condition of his rule that he shall spend his life trying to impress the "natives" and so in every crisis he has got to do what the "natives" expect of him. He wears a mask, and his face grows to fit it. I had got to shoot the elephant. I had committed myself to doing it when I sent for the rifle. A sahib has got to act like a sahib; he has got to appear resolute, to know his own mind and do definite things. To come all that way, rifle in hand, with two thousand people marching at my heels, and then to trail feebly away, having done nothing – no, that was impossible.

'The crowd would laugh at me. And my whole life, every white man's life in the East, was one long struggle not to be laughed at.

'But I did not want to shoot the elephant. I watched him beating his bunch of grass against his knees, with that preoccupied grandmotherly air that elephants have. It seemed to me that it would be murder to shoot him. At that age I was not squeamish about killing animals, but I had never shot an elephant and never wanted to. (Somehow it always seems worse to kill a *large* animal.) Besides, there was the beast's owner to be considered. Alive, the elephant was worth at least a hundred pounds; dead he would only be worth the value of his tusks – five pounds possibly. But I had got to act quickly. I turned to some experienced-looking Burmans who had been there when we arrived, and asked them how the elephant had been behaving. They all said the same thing: he took no notice of you if you left him alone, but he might charge if you went too close to him.

'It was perfectly clear to me what I ought to do. I ought to walk up to within, say, twenty-five yards of the elephant and test his behaviour. If he charged I could shoot, if he took no notice of me it would be safe to leave him until the mahout came back. But also I knew that I was going to do no such thing. I was a poor shot with a rifle and the ground was soft mud into which one would sink at every step. If the elephant charged and I missed him, I should have about as much chance as a toad under a steamroller. But even then I was not thinking particularly of my own skin, only the watchful yellow faces behind. For at that moment, with the crowd watching me, I was not afraid in the ordinary sense, as I would have been if I had been alone. A white man mustn't be frightened in front of the "natives"; and so, in general, he isn't frightened. The sole thought in my mind was that if anything went wrong those two thousand Burmans would see me pursued, caught, trampled on and reduced to a grinning corpse like that Indian up the hill. And if that happened it was quite probable that some of them would laugh. That would never do. There was only one alternative. I shoved the cartridges into the magazine and lay down on the road to get a better aim.'

George Orwell *Shooting an Elephant* 1957

1 Why did Orwell not want to shoot the elephant?

2 What alternatives were there to shooting it?

3 Orwell describes himself as a 'puppet pushed to and fro'. 'A sahib,' he wrote, 'has got to act like a sahib'. What were the things a sahib should, or should not, do in acting out the role?

4 Can you think of any other occasions where the pressure of the group might influence the behaviour of the individual?

5 How might the following sociological terms be used to explain the incident Orwell describes?
role
status
norm
social control
actor
identity
group pressure

13
Cake factory

Speech is such an obvious form of communication that we often forget that we communicate to others in many different ways. The clothes we wear, the expression on our faces, gestures and body movements all communicate meanings to other people. Communications which convey meanings are described as symbols.

Working in a cake factory Polly Toynbee discovered that many actions can be symbolic.

Quarrels flare up quickly, for no apparent reason. A tiny old man sat like a small bundle on a high stool, feeding the ready creamed cakes into a machine that cut them into four. He suddenly started to yell and scream, louder than the machines, at a tall African girl who was putting the cakes from a trolley on to the belt for him. She screamed back at him. Neither could hear what the other was saying. Eventually the supervisor came and bawled out both of them. Later, at lunch, the girl told me that he'd been complaining to her that she was putting the cakes out too fast or too slow, and that she never did it right. 'He's always on at me,' she said. 'Nothing I bloody do is right.'

When she said, 'He's always on at me,' she didn't mean that he actually said anything, because he wouldn't have been heard. All communication is non-verbal, but it's communication all the same. She meant that he'd been angry with her, that he'd been glowering at her, grabbing the cakes away from her before she had let go, taking the cakes especially fast to show that she was going slower than he wanted her to go. She had got angry and gone slower still, not seeing any reason for speeding up, had held on to each cake a fraction of a second too long, had given a slightly diffident look around the room while languidly handing out the next one, pretending not to notice that he wanted to go faster. And all this was practically unnoticeable to anyone not working on that particular line at that particular time. It is such a fractionally small delay, or speeding up, that an observer couldn't see it or time it.

I found myself being maddened with rage by the woman sitting opposite me. She was a large, rather sour middle aged West Indian. She had been there for years, and was controlling the flow of the cream machine. It was also her job to put the top layer of the cake on to the second layer, as it came out of the machine. I had to lift both layers and put them on to the third. As we sat opposite one another, the speed at which she worked determined the rate at which I had to work. As she did her bit first, it meant that I had to do mine later, and a little further down. If she was slow, or held on to the cake for an extra moment, I had to lean further down the line, which was uncomfortable and she knew it. We never spoke a word, but there was a great deal of aggression between us. She would hold on to the cakes longer and longer, and sometimes I would even have to get up and walk down the line to catch up. We also had to clean up the spare cream that often came out on to the belt. She was quicker than me with the palette knife and would clean up my bit, too. Then I would get better at it and poach on to her bit. The point of this was that sometimes no cream came out of the machine, and we had to spread it ourselves from the cream in the bowl beside us. The cream in the bowl was the spare cream we had gleaned off the belt, so we had to collect as much of it as we could.

All this sounds insane. Of course it is, and it is what preoccupies everyone in assembly line work. Ask what we were thinking – we were thinking about how infuriating the person we worked with was, or we were waiting for the next bit of spare cream to spill on to the conveyor belt. Mad, obsessive, and utterly pointless. If the work is of minimal interest, so the thoughts and preoccupations of the mind will match it exactly. A stupid boring job makes a stupid boring mind.

Polly Toynbee *A Working Life* 1971

1 What did the girl mean by saying 'He's always on at me' when the old man had not actually said anything? How had he communicated his anger?

2 How did she respond to his signs of annoyance? What effect did this have?

3 How did the woman sitting opposite control the way Polly Toynbee had to work?

4 Make a list of all the actions and gestures listed in the extract. Alongside each action or gesture write down what it might have meant to both the person making

it and the person to whom it was made.

5 Observe an ordinary situation – a school assembly, a bus conductor collecting fares, people queuing in a supermarket, a family meal – and see how many examples of symbolic action you can spot.

14

The Samoan family

Margaret Mead was a social anthropologist who spent many years of her life studying simple communities in many parts of the world. In this extract from *Coming of Age in Samoa* she describes the family relationships on the Pacific island of Samoa.

A Samoan village is made up of some thirty to forty households, each of which is presided over by a headman called a *matai*. These headmen hold either chiefly titles or the titles of talking chiefs, who are the official orators, spokesmen, and ambassadors of chiefs. In a formal village assembly each *matai* has his place, and represents and is responsible for all the members of his household. These households include all the individuals who live for any length of time under the authority and protection of a common *matai*. Their composition varies from the biological family consisting of parents and children only, to households of fifteen and twenty people who are all related to the *matai* or to his wife by blood, marriage, or adoption, but who often have no close relationship to each other. The adopted members of a household are usually but not necessarily distant relatives.

Widows and widowers, especially when they are childless, usually return to their blood relatives, but a married couple may live with the relatives of either one. Such a household is not necessarily a close residential unit, but may be scattered over the village in three or four houses. No one living permanently in another village is counted as a member of the household, which is strictly a local unit. Economically, the household is also a unit, for all work upon the plantations is under the supervision of the *matai*, who in turn parcels out to them food and other necessities.

Within the household, age rather than relationship gives disciplinary authority. The *matai* exercises nominal and usually real authority over every individual under his protection, even over his father and mother. This control is, of course, modified by personality difference, always carefully tempered, however, by a ceremonious acknowledgement of his position. The newest baby born into such a household is subject to every individual in it, and his position improves no whit with age until a younger child appears upon the scene. But in most households the position of youngest is a highly temporary one. Nieces and nephews or destitute young cousins come to swell the ranks of the household, and at adolescence a girl stands virtually in the middle with as many individuals who must obey her as there are persons to whom she owes obedience. Where increased efficiency and increased self-consciousness would perhaps have made her obstreperous and restless in a differently organised family, here she has ample outlet for a growing sense of authority.

This development is perfectly regular. A girl's marriage makes a minimum of difference in this respect, except in so far as her own children increase most pertinently the supply of agreeably docile subordinates. But the girls who remain unmarried even beyond their early twenties are in no wise less highly regarded or less responsible than their married sisters. This tendency to make the classifying principle age rather than married state, is reinforced outside the home by the fact that the wives of untitled men and all unmarried girls past puberty are classed together in the ceremonial organisation of the village.

Relatives in other households also play a role in the children's lives. Any older relative has a right to demand personal service from younger relatives, a right to criticise their conduct and to interfere in their affairs. Thus a little girl may escape alone down to the beach to bathe only to be met by an older cousin who sets her washing or caring for a baby or to fetch some coconut to scrub the clothes. So closely is the daily life bound up with this universal servitude and so numerous are the acknowledged relationships in the name of which service can be exacted, that for the children an hour's escape from surveillance is almost impossible.

This loose but demanding relationship group has its compensations also. Within it a child of three can wander safely and come to no harm, can be sure of finding food and drink, a sheet to wrap herself up in for a nap, a kind hand to dry casual tears and bind up her wounds. Any small children who are missing when night falls, are simply 'sought among their kinsfolk', and a baby whose mother has gone inland to work on the plantation is passed from hand to hand for the length of the village.

Margaret Mead *Coming of Age in Samoa* 1943

1 What is meant by the following terms?
a biological family
b household
c adolescence
d economic unit

2 Make a list of all of the people whom you might find in a Samoan household. At the top of your list you should put the *matai* and his wife. Would you include all of these people in 'the family' in Britain?

3 What determines the individual's status in the Samoan household?

4 What does Margaret Mead mean when she writes, 'at adolescence a girl stands virtually in the middle with as many individuals who must obey her as there are persons to whom she owes obedience.' Give examples from the extract.

5 In what ways is the position of the teenage girl in Samoa different from that of a young person in a British family today?

6 Children in Samoa are treated very differently in comparison to young children in Britain. Make a list of the differences.

15

The slow march

How has family life changed in the last two hundred years? What has caused the changes and what have been their consequences?

The process of change has so far proceeded through three stages. In the first stage, the pre-industrial, the family was usually the unit of production. For the most part, men, women and children worked together in home and field. This type of economic partnership was, for working class people, supplanted after a bitter struggle by the stage 2 family, whose members were caught up in the new economy as individual wage-earners.

The process affected most the families of manual workers (and not all of these by any means). The trends were different in the middle class family, where the contrasts for both husbands and wives were somewhat less sharp than they had been in the past. But as working class people were preponderant most families were probably 'torn apart' by the new economic system. In the third stage the unity of the family has been restored around its functions as the unit not of production but of consumption.

The stage 1 family lasted until the new industry overran it in a rolling advance which went on from the eighteenth well into the nineteenth century. The development of the new industry was uneven as between different parts of the country, coming much later to London than to the industrial north. It also outmoded the old techniques of production more slowly in some occupations than others. But come it did, eventually, along with many other forms of employment which shared one vital feature, that the employees worked for wages. This led to the stage 2 family. The third stage started earlier in the twentieth century and is still working its way downwards. At any one period there were, and still are, families representing all three stages. But as first one stage and then another has been set in motion, the proportions in stage 2 increased in the nineteenth century and in stage 3 in the twentieth.

The new kind of family has three main characteristics which differentiate it from the sort which prevailed in stage 2. The first is that the couple, and their children, are very much centred on the home, especially when the children are young. They can be so much together, and share so much together, because they spend so much of their time together in the same space. Life has, to use another term, become more 'privatised'.

The second characteristic is that the extended family (consisting of relatives of several different degrees to some extent sharing a common life) counts for less and the immediate, or nuclear, family for more. We have not been able to discover much documentary evidence about kinship patterns in nineteenth century England. People certainly often lived with or near relatives, and we would expect that daughters more often maintained close links with their parents, and particularly with their mothers, than sons did with theirs. Extended families must have been used for mutual aid. But we doubt whether they became so pervasive and so much the arena of women's lives until this century. Our belief is that since the second war, in particular, there has been a further change and that the nuclear family has become relatively more isolated in the working as in other classes.

The third and most vital characteristic is that inside the family of marriage the roles of the sexes have become less segregated.

Michael Young and Peter Willmott *The Symmetrical Family* 1975

1 What do you understand by the following terms?
a pre-industrial
b unit of consumption
c privatised
d extended family
e nuclear family
f symmetrical
g segregated roles

2 How did the change from a pre-industrial society, based largely on farming, to an industrial society based on factory industry, affect families.

3 These changes in family life are still continuing. Which stage are we at now?

4 The stage 3 family has three characteristics:
a it is 'privatised';
b it is nuclear;
c it involves less segregation of roles.
In your own words describe the type of family you would expect to find at stage 3. How close does your family come to this type?

5 Collect pictures from newspapers and magazines which you feel would illustrate the way of life of the stage 3 family.

6 This extract comes from the beginning of a book entitled *The Symmetrical Family*. Which of these three stages of family is 'symmetrical'? Explain why.

16

Children of working mothers

The National Child Development Study followed the early lives of nearly 16,000 children born during one week in March 1958. By the time the children reached the age of seven a vast amount of information had been collected on their physical and emotional development, their family backgrounds, progress at school and many other factors. The amount of evidence collected enabled them to comment on a number of issues including the children of working mothers.

For most of this century, apart from increases in times of war, women have constituted about one-third of the work force, a figure which is rising slowly but not startlingly. What is rising fast is the proportion of women workers who are married. Many social commentators have greeted this increase with dismay largely because of its alleged effect upon children.

The assumption behind this attitude is that children will develop best if their mother's time is spent in the home and on the family rather than on paid work outside the home; and that if the mother does work, the older the child is when she starts, the better it is for that child. This view was echoed in a study by Goodacre, who asked teachers what they considered were desirable home conditions. A non-working mother was mentioned in a high proportion of answers.

Not all public comment agrees with this view; a definite note of protest underlies these remarks of a writer in the *Guardian*: 'At least once a week, inspired by anything from equal pay for women to a particularly juvenile delinquent, some judge, MP, professor, psychiatrist, rector or proctor can be counted upon to rise, accuse the working mother and advocate renewed effort in promoting home-making as a talent.'

Home-making probably strikes most people as a 'talent' worth promoting but is it necessarily incompatible with working? Perhaps there are dangers in overemphasising the needs of the home and the family. Certainly some observers warn that there are dangers in fulltime motherhood: Rossi, for example: 'I suspect that the things women do for and with their children have been needlessly elaborated to make motherhood a full-time job. Unfortunately, in this very process the child's struggle for autonomy and independence, for privacy and the right to worry things through for himself, are subtly reduced by the omnipresent mother.'

Here, then, is a controversy about children's development, the implications of which are both social and economic. Are there any facts with which to augment the hearsay evidence? What support may the protagonists discover in research findings? Stolz concluded that the results were so contradictory that almost any point of view could find some support. The lack of any consensus was attributed to the failure of the research workers to take account fully – if at all – of the relevant factors. These would include, for example, social class, family size, the age of the child, the duration of the work and the standard of alternative care.

Clearly, failure to take account of these factors could lead to conflicting results. For example, analysis of our results showed that working mothers were more in evidence in the less skilled social class groups, so that on this basis their children might be expected to compare unfavourably in school performance with those of non-working mothers. Secondly, however, working mothers tended to have *smaller* families and, as has been shown, children from small families do *better* at school than those in large families. Thirdly, although this was not specifically examined, it seemed reasonable to assume that the group of working mothers would more often contain widows and wives separated from their husbands. Again, it has been shown that children living in atypical parental situations are at some disadvantage educationally.

However, it is clear that, in general, the children of working mothers do not show any marked ill effects at the age of seven in terms of their attainment and adjustment in school. It may be that any important ill effects will manifest themselves at later ages but this seems unlikely since a younger child is more vulnerable to environmental and other stresses. It may also be that the children's behaviour or adjustment at home suffers and this must for the moment remain an open question.

Ronald Davie, Neville Butler and Harvie Goldstein *From Birth to Seven* 1972

Table 1   Women in the labour force 1951–75

Women:	1951		1961		1971		1975	
	million	%	million	%	million	%	million	%
married	2.7	**12.0**	3.9	**16.5**	5.8	**23.0**	6.6	**25.5**
others	4.3	**19.0**	3.9	**16.5**	3.4	**13.5**	3.2	**12.5**
total	7.0	**31.0**	7.7	**33.0**	9.2	**36.5**	9.8	**38.0**
Men	15.6	**69.0**	16.1	**67.0**	15.9	**63.5**	15.8	**62.0**
Total	22.6	**100**	23.8	**100**	25.1	**100**	25.6	**100**

(*Adapted from Social Trends 1980*)

1 What assumptions have been made about a child's development and how the mother spends her time?

2 Comment on the following statements saying whether you agree or disagree, and why.
a Children of working mothers generally do less well at school.
b More middle class mothers are likely to work.
c Mothers who go out to work are more likely to have big families and this is why they work.
d Mothers may have to go out to work because they have an inadequate income as a result of divorce or widowhood which could have an effect on the child's emotional development.

17
The family under capitalism

Karl Marx believed the industrial revolution would lead to important changes in the family and in the relationships between the sexes. In his view industrialisation would give women and young people new freedoms outside of the home. Capitalism would, he argued, sweep away 'the economical basis of parental authority'. Sheila Rowbotham suggests that something rather different has happened.

The assumption Marx expressed in *Capital* – that the industrial revolution laid a 'new economical foundation for a higher form of the family, and of the relation between the sexes', because it assigned an important part in 'the process of production, outside the domestic sphere, to women, to young persons, and to children of both sexes', and that thus the 'capitalistic mode of exploitation' swept away 'the economical basis of parental authority' – has remained only partially correct. He seemed to think that the family would simply be swept away along with other pre-capitalist preserves. Other factors have intervened to make the whole process more complicated. The family was supplemented rather than dissolved. Already in the nineteenth century the state had begun to take over certain aspects of the authority of individual families. The introduction of the factory acts meant that husbands could not benefit from their wives working in certain jobs, any more than parents could from their children's labour. The growth of compulsory education meant that parents retained economic control over their children but were answerable to the state legally if they kept them away from school. The pressure for these developments came from a varied lobby, from humane upper class philanthropists, concerned about the destruction of old family ties and the horrors of the early stages of industrial revolution, from male workers concerned for their jobs, from the growing power of the labour movement, and finally from the needs of capitalism itself. As technology produced more and more complex machines in the twentieth century there was a need for a work force with some basic education. Similarly, industrialisation demanded disciplined workers, broken in at an early age to specific modes of production and consumption. Schools for the working class developed round these narrow requirements of capitalist production. Legislation relating to children, child care, and family allowances have extended the state's intervention.

Despite these changes in capitalism, there was no need to alter fundamentally the division of labour between the sexes. The capitalist state has kept women morally responsible for children. Rather than turn the family into a rationalised part of commodity production, a baby farm with paid employees and no sentiment, it is both immediately more profitable and more politically convenient to utilise the accepted idea that women maintain the family outside the cash-nexus or at the lowest conceivable rate granted by the family allowance or social security. The continuance of such a state of affairs is directly linked to the unequal exploitation of female labour in industry.

The conflict Marx noted between work at home and in commodity production, the physical impossibility of women doing both, has not

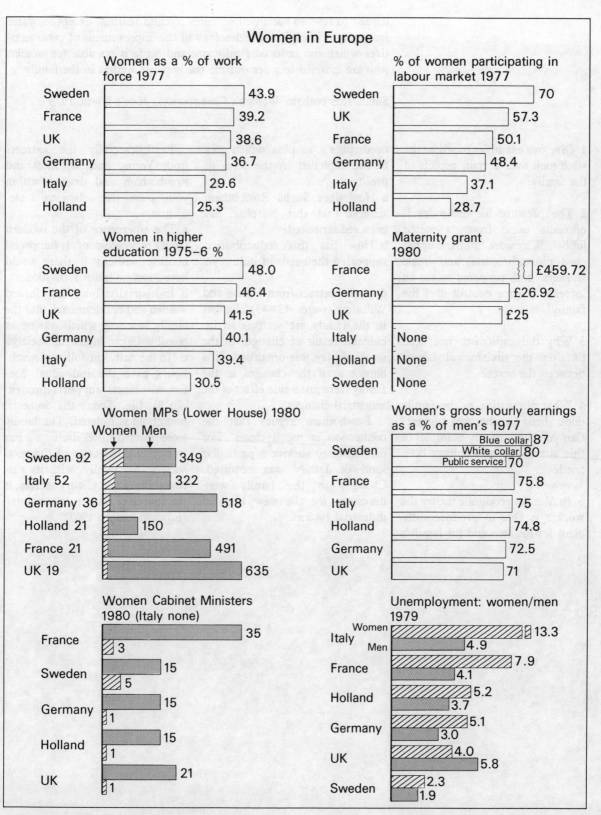

Women in Europe

Women as a % of work force 1977
Sweden	43.9
France	39.2
UK	38.6
Germany	36.7
Italy	29.6
Holland	25.3

% of women participating in labour market 1977
Sweden	70
UK	57.3
France	50.1
Germany	48.4
Italy	37.1
Holland	28.7

Women in higher education 1975–6 %
Sweden	48.0
France	46.4
UK	41.5
Germany	40.1
Italy	39.4
Holland	30.5

Maternity grant 1980
France	£459.72
Germany	£26.92
UK	£25
Italy	None
Holland	None
Sweden	None

Women MPs (Lower House) 1980
Women Men
	Women	Men
Sweden	92	349
Italy	52	322
Germany	36	518
Holland	21	150
France	21	491
UK	19	635

Women's gross hourly earnings as a % of men's 1977
Sweden	Blue collar 87
	White collar 80
	Public service 70
France	75.8
Italy	75
Holland	74.8
Germany	72.5
UK	71

Women Cabinet Ministers 1980 (Italy none)
France	35
	3
Sweden	15
	5
Germany	15
	1
Holland	15
	1
UK	21
	1

Unemployment: women/men 1979
	Women	Men
Italy	13.3	4.9
France	7.9	4.1
Holland	5.2	3.7
Germany	5.1	3.0
UK	4.0	5.8
Sweden	2.3	1.9

Adapted from *The Guardian* 30 June 1980

tended to lead to socialised schemes of child rearing, except in wars. Ironically it is capitalist technology in the improvement of contraceptives which has reduced family size and made it possible for women who are married to work outside the home as well as in the family.

Sheila Rowbotham *Woman's Consciousness, Man's World* 1973

1 Give two examples of where the state took over certain aspects of the family?

2 The pressure for these developments came from 'a varied lobby'. Why were 'humane upper class philanthropists' and 'male workers' both prepared to see an increase in state control over the family?

3 Why did capitalism not need to alter the division of labour between the sexes?

4 What alternative to the family does Sheila Rowbotham suggest? Can you think of any examples of this alternative which have been tried?

5 In Marxist economic theory the worker is able to produce sufficient for his own and his family's needs plus a 'surplus' which goes to the capitalist in the form of profit.
a How does Sheila Rowbotham suggest that this 'surplus' has been redistributed?
b How has this redistribution supported the needs of industry?

6 In the extract from Young and Willmott (pages 42–43) changes in the family are seen as an incidental result of changes in the way industry was organised. It is almost as if the changes in the family were just a side effect of the industrial changes.

Rowbotham argues that the connection is much closer. For capitalism to survive a particular kind of family was required. Changes in the family were necessary for the new kind of industrial system.

Read carefully the extracts from Young and Willmott and Rowbotham and discuss within your class the following statements:
a The emergence of the modern family is no accident. It happened because without it there could have been no industrialisation.
b Industrialisation has forced women and children back into the family in a way which was never possible in pre-industrial society.
c 'In the past, kinsfolk and neighbours gave the individual continuous moral support throughout his life. Today the domestic household is isolated. The family looks inward upon itself . . . Far from being the basis of the good society, the family, with its narrow privacy and tawdry secrets, is the source of all our discontents.' (Edward Leach, 1967)

18
The school that I'd like

The Observer newspaper ran an essay competition on the subject 'The school that I'd like'. This is one of the winning entries.

The infant and primary schools are considered unimportant (compared to other ages), and so school is allowed to be interesting. As we get older our school life becomes less and less interesting as our teachers attempt to cram us with as much knowledge as possible for the exams. He passes or fails it – and forgets all about it. Exams are good as objective methods of finding how much one knows, but there is more to life than exams.

Apparently a boy is not supposed to have any natural curiosity for school subjects, and the way they are taught it is quite true. Attempts to induce learning by prizes, stars, etc., fail because learning is not competitive.

Teaching machines can be put to good use, but indiscriminate use makes them boring and ignored. For some things a teacher is indispensable. A teacher may also introduce discussion and humour, although more often than not we laugh at, and not with, him.

I object to corporal punishment, but even more to the casual clouts handed out for reasons as unfair as a teacher's anxiety or for a pupil just not understanding. Corporal punishment is brutal and degrading. We boys are thinking, often mature, human beings. I have seen a teacher hit a boy hard and say, 'Don't bully! – it will only make him bully more. The learning induced by it will be quickly forgotten, and the subjects hated evermore. Moreover, with better-adjusted teachers we become unmanageable as a sort of recompense, and they, too, may resort to corporal punishment. It also produces senseless flouting of school rules.

The pitiful thing is that the prefects have now forgotten the lower form boy's point of view and punish him as they were punished.

As for the number of senseless rules made up by the school – we ignore them. This brings risk of ignoring sensible rules.

My main complaint is that we have so little say in school affairs. Naturally the boys who are allowed most say are those who have conformed to school ideals and regulations. Most boys just ignore our 'school duty' and when ordered to pick up litter for the glory of the school, just sit down and pick daisies. We are all expected to be devoutly religious, and atheism is in no way recognised. While one can complain at a serious offence, there is no defence for a boy 'picked on' by a teacher.

On the whole there is less need for radical changes in school organisation – it makes little difference if lessons are held under a tree or in a skyscraper. It appears large schools are inevitable, but anonymity could be dispelled by good teacher–boy–parent relations (if possible informal). Widened horizons are provided by athletic 'houses', with chances for boys of all specialities to mix.

I believe in co-educational schools because life is co-educational.

Maths has always been taught so drearily, especially when it is so important. Some pupils are even set long sums as punishment!

To sum up – the average boy goes to school, becomes bored, gets into mischief, is punished, 'takes it out' on other boys, is crammed with knowledge for the exams, passes or fails his exams, forgets and has learnt to hate that subject through bad teaching.

The average teacher (even the idealistic sort) has to force much knowledge on boys, tries teaching without punishment, boys 'take it out' on him for the vicious masters, he becomes a vicious master.

So, basically, make the subject a joy to learn, interesting and worthwhile; cut out force; give us a say in the school.

You must remember that I have discounted all the friendliness and humour of boy and teacher – but the school system tries to do this too. There is more to school than academic results.

Edward Blishen *The School that I'd like 1969*

1 What is this writer's view of exams or 'school knowledge'?

2 How is learning made competitive?

3 The writer is critical of corporal punishment. Why?

4 What evidence is there in the essay that particular ways of educating can be reproduced from one generation to another?

5 Sociologists have used the term 'hidden curriculum' to describe those things that are learned at school other than the school subjects themselves. What do you think this boy has learned from his school life?

6 What do you think he means when he concludes: 'There is more to school than academic results'?

"*First day at Grammar School and he's a pillar of the establishment*"

19
'Please Miss'

People learn at a very young age what behaviour is appropriate and what isn't. Teachers' actual behaviour in classrooms needs to fit in with the expectations of other teachers and of the pupils. Quite often the behaviour that is expected from teachers is very different from the behaviour they were taught in college. Derek Hanson and Margaret Herrington studied how a group of student teachers learned the expectations their pupils had of them.

Teachers become the way they are because the pupils teach them what to do. This is more important than, for example, what student teachers are taught at college. So, at least, we concluded from a study of a small group of would-be teachers. As teachers their attitudes and behaviour were shaped by what they thought their pupils expected of them – and by what the pupils did to bring teachers into line.

The expectations, of course, varied according to age group. And it is necessary to distinguish what pupils *like* in teachers from what they *expect*. These expectations have been learned from experiences at school, and from parents, friends, comics or television.

Primary school children, our study suggested, don't like teachers who shout at them, or who are sarcastic, impatient or uninterested in their work. Popular teachers are kind, tactful, approachable and apparently competent. But what is soon clear is that most of these children expect the teacher to act as the boss; to direct, initiate and control learning; to be judge and jury of work and conduct; and to act according to his status in the school. It is these expectations, rather than likes or dislikes, which are most apparent:

'Is this handwriting all right, miss?'
'What do you think, John?'
'It seems all right to me.'
'Then why ask me?'
'Because you are the teacher: you are supposed to say if it's good and write "good" at the bottom.'
Or: 'Please Miss, Dawn is eating.'
'What's that got to do with me?'
'Please Miss, you are the teacher, you are supposed to stop her.'
'Does it worry you if she's eating?'
'No Miss, but Mr Brown says we haven't to eat sweets on the bus.'
'So this seems to be a matter between you, Dawn, and Mr Brown to settle. Where do I come in?'
'Because Mr Brown is the headteacher and you have to do what he says.'
Seven year old pupils learn the reality of grading and grouping and feel the need to put the probationer teacher right:
'Please Miss, I need some half sheets of paper.'
'Why?'
'To give those boys over there. They are only supposed to get small sheets.'
'Why is that?'
'Because they don't do much work, Miss.'

'So perhaps they need full sheets so they can catch up with the rest of you?' (No reply from the monitor inevitably one of the good girls in the class and a possible future teacher.)

Or: 'That's a lovely fish. Who made that?'

'Please Miss, Keith.'

'Then Keith must be very clever.'

'Oh no, Miss; Keith isn't a bit clever. He can't do his sums.'

We followed the experience of our 16 new teachers (including three mature students) in great detail, by discussion and reports. We found that even top juniors, who have experienced the annual ritual of decorating the classroom for Christmas for the past six years, expect the teacher to organise them, tell them what to do and control the operation. They reveal deep unease if they are given the materials and told to get on with it. What they have learned is that decorating a classroom is overlaid with heavy meanings; that it is an annual competition among teachers as to who can 'put on the best display'. Their new, uninformed and ignorant teacher has to be trained correctly or both they and she will come bottom in the league table. So, 'Please Miss, you tell us what to do.'

Derek Hanson and Margaret Herrington *Please Miss, you're supposed to stop her* 1978

1 How do pupils learn to know what to expect from teachers?

2 What are the characteristics of:
a a popular primary school teacher?
b an unpopular primary school teacher?

3 The pupils whose words are recorded in the extract are creating a role for the teacher. What sort of role is it?

4 Is there any evidence in the extract that the pupils have also created roles for themselves? Give examples.

5 In what ways did the student teachers whose words are recorded say the 'wrong things'. Give examples.

6 An American sociologist Harold Garfinkle developed a method of 'disrupting' the way people took situations for granted. He suggested that individuals could go into a social situation and behave as if they had no knowledge of the appropriate behaviour. The student teachers have begun to do this in this extract.

Write an imaginary conversation between a teacher and a class in which the teacher does not know what is expected in that situation.

20
The comprehensive school

Paul Bellaby, writing in 1976, outlines the development of comprehensive education and some of the problems of determining how much progress has been made.

There are many questions to ask about comprehensive schooling, but first we must discuss the meaning of the term.

In England, its most obvious meaning is the abolition of the selection of children at 11 plus for separate grammar and secondary modern schools, and the establishment of secondary schools attended by children of all abilities. Soon after the 1944 Education Act, which made possible the extension of 'secondary' education to all up to fifteen years of age, a few schools were founded on the comprehensive model, but most were either grammar schools selecting the top 20 per cent at eleven, or the new secondary moderns who received the remainder. Within the broad national picture, there were many local variations. In some Welsh education authorities, two in five children at eleven would be sent to grammar school; some English authorities catered for fewer than one in five. The influential Norwood Report of 1943 envisaged a tripartite system of selective grammar, selective technical and non-selective modern schools, each dealing with children of a different aptitude ('academic', 'technical', and 'practical'). While the provision of grammar school places was general, only a minority of education authorities established technical schools, chiefly in larger urban areas. Variation in provision was in some respects also *inequality*. The campaign to reorganise secondary schooling stems from the middle 1950s. The Labour leadership did not make comprehensive education firm policy until the early 1960s. But after it returned to power in 1964 (for the first time since 1951) it put pressure on local authorities to prepare plans for reorganisation. Though apparently impeded by a period of Conservative rule (1970–74), the reform has in fact continued gradually, without state legislation to enforce it, since 1964/65.

The graph illustrates the progress of comprehensive schooling in England and Wales between 1950 and 1974, the last date for which statistics are currently available. Comprehensive schooling began to lift off during the Conservative government between 1951 and 1964, though it was not until the late fifties and early sixties, the period

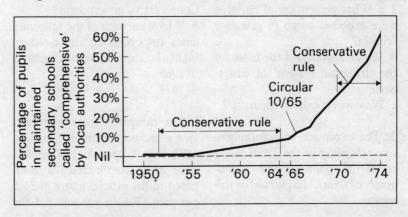

associated with the post-war baby boom or 'bulge' in the secondary school intake, that local authorities and the Ministry were prepared to extend experiments with this form of school organisation. The impact of the Labour government's famous circular 10/65 is readily seen. Mrs Thatcher's much criticised handling of local authority reorganisation plans between 1970 and 1974 (when she was Minister of Education in the Conservative government) did not seem to slacken the pace of reform. In the course of 1973 the halfway mark was passed, that is more than 50 per cent of children of secondary school age in the maintained sector were attending comprehensive schools (including a small number in middle schools of 10–13 age range).

However, the official statistics on which the graph is based have to be interpreted with care. In its survey of comprehensive reorganisation in 1971, the Campaign for Comprehensive Education reduced the official figure for that year (36.5 per cent) to as little as 12 per cent by specifying more rigorous standards for use of the term comprehensive. One and a half per cent in middle schools were left out. Schools in schemes that were still selective (for example at the age of transfer from the first to the second level secondary schools), schools that practised selection among themselves, and those that coexisted with grammar schools in their catchment areas, made up the majority of those remaining, and these too were excluded to reach the figure of 12 per cent in 'fully comprehensive' education. Even this exercise was not as rigorous as some might have wished. Comprehensive schools frequently (even *normally*) practise selection *internally*: only a quarter in 1972 had even a degree of mixed ability grouping in the early years, while most also selected for 'O' level and CSE streams after thirteen or fourteen and on entry to the sixth form. If one defined 'comprehensive' by the *absence of selection by academic ability* there would be few schools to include in the graph, even now.

Paul Bellaby *The Sociology of Comprehensive Schooling* 1977

1 Give one definition of 'comprehensive schooling'.

2 a What percentage of children were expected to go to grammar schools?
b Which report laid the basis for the 'tripartite system' of education?
c Why was it called 'tripartite'?

3 'The expansion of comprehensive schooling in the 1960s was a result of political and demographic factors.' Explain what this means.

4 a Is it true that the growth in comprehensive schooling has been slower during periods of Conservative government?
b Why were each of the following dates important in the development of comprehensive schooling?
i 1965
ii 1973

5 The campaign for comprehensive education estimated that in 1971 only 12 per cent of schools were truly 'comprehensive' compared to the official figure of 36.5 per cent. Which schools did the campaign for comprehensive education claim were not truly comprehensive?

6 Bellaby is critical of schools which 'practise selection internally'. The most common form of 'internal selection' are:
a streaming
b setting
c banding.
What is the difference between each of these methods of 'internal selection'?

21
Education and inequality

Inequality in education has been an important theme for sociological and psychological debate for a very long time. In the 1950s and 1960s the sociology of education was dominated by a search for the causes of inequality and for social policies which would remove them. In this extract William Tyler outlines the main areas of inequality.

What is educational inequality? When people speak of inequality in education they may mean several things. They may mean, for example, that some children can read better than others for their age, and are more likely to stay on at school and go on to university. They may mean, on the other hand, that some children come from families that give them certain advantages such as encyclopaedias, visits to art galleries and museums and help with their homework. A possible, though perhaps more unusual, meaning could be that some children are able to read at higher levels than others of the same age because they were born that way. In this case any advantage would be a natural or innate one.

More often than not, however, educational inequality is about the advantages that come from different experiences and stimulation that the school provides. Some people believe that sending a child to a fee-paying school will give him a headstart in life. Because of the 'better' or more academic educational climate of the school it is claimed that the child will learn faster, stay on longer and pick up credentials that will increase his lifetime earnings. On the non-academic side it is believed that such a child may be more likely to make friends who in later life could help him to obtain a high status and well-paying occupation.

Let us go through these different meanings of educational inequality again and give each of them the term that is used by writers in this field. The first kind of inequality is that of *achievement*, as shown in different levels of competence or skill in school subjects such as reading, arithmetic or knowledge of history or geography. The second refers to inequality in educational *background*, usually in the family which in turn may be related to the neighbourhood, the occupational group of the father, the region or an ethnic group. The third inequality is that of *aptitude* or *ability*, that is of potential for learning. Although many would disagree with the claim that this is inborn, there is no doubt that it remains fairly constant after a certain age. The fourth type of inequality is that of *school environment*. This is the area that is most hotly discussed and debated because it is the one that people feel is both most important and most easily removed. It may refer to the type of teaching, facilities or curriculum that the school offers, or it may refer to its non-academic advantages – its 'snob' appeal – reflected in the manners, the accent and the social standing of the child's friendship group.

The two remaining types of inequality are concerned with tangible outcomes of education. First of all there are *credentials* which are indicated by the level and quality of examination results, or simply by a piece of paper to prove that an individual has attended an institution for a certain period of time. Finally there are *life chances* which refer here specifically to status and income. These are to a large extent influenced by the type, quality and duration of schooling one has received. Some sociologists claim that this influence is increasing and that most of the differences between people will soon be almost entirely determined by their educational success. This is sometimes called 'educational stratification' and is believed by many writers to be a necessary characteristic of modern society.

It may appear then that it is very difficult to use the term 'educational inequality' because it can refer to so many things – potential, opportunity, outcomes and rewards. This should not disturb us, however, since writers in education or in sociology usually make it clear which type of inequality they are referring to. What is more important than the particular uses of the term are the relationships that are implied and direction of a writer's bias in *explaining* one particular kind of inequality. In fact, it is almost impossible to use the term 'educational inequality' in one sense without at the same time implying how it may be related to or connected with all the others.

William Tyler *The Sociology of Educational Inequality* 1977

1 What are the six types of educational inequality outlined by William Tyler?

2 Give a brief description of each type of inequality.

3 Read the following statements. To which of Tyler's 'inequalities' does each refer?
a 'Trainee wanted. Must have GCE 'O' Level or CSE (1) in Maths and English.'
b 'Joan was born clever.'

c 'They never did very well at school, not from an area like that.'
d 'He was a hard worker who made it by his own efforts.'
e 'He went to a good school you know, he was bound to get on.'
f 'Her father owned the firm so she was sure to get a good start.'

"Some people would blame your genes, others your home environment, but I blame you, Wimpole, plain and simple."

22

Schools for privilege

How can private schools help you get on in life? *New Society* writer, Joanna Mack, spoke to teachers and boys at Westminster School.

'I suppose I'll end up being a barrister like my father. It's always rather assumed I'm going to be one, or some sort of lawyer. It's quite a worthwhile job, father enjoys it.' This 14 year old public schoolboy's father is a Queen's Counsel – 'about fourth from the top,' says the son. Uncle and godfather are high up in the legal profession. 'Father has lots of influential friends, it certainly might help. I've got a friend whose father was a high court judge and he was already a right honourable at about 35.' I asked this pupil of Westminster School whether it would worry him if he felt he had advanced because of his father's position. 'Worry me?' he replied, looking puzzled. 'I think it would be quite fine.'

Public schools may not be in the news at the moment, but public schoolboys inevitably are. Which of us can recall a time when it was not so? The old boys' influence, public and private, is way out of proportion to their numbers. Westminster School, founded in 1560 with fine buildings and quiet cloisters, in the shadow of the abbey, takes about 500 boys (just over half are boarders) and in the last few years about 40 sixth form girls.

Most of the eleven second year boys gathered in the school's precisely furnished reception room backed up the future lawyer. Nivad Shah argued, 'Pulling strings is one of the only ways you can succeed. Otherwise it's going to be really difficult.' Mathew Baker who sees his own future in the army, feels: 'Civilisation works like that. It's happened all through British history.'

Independent schools remain politically controversial because the children of parents who can afford the fees seem – at least on the surface – to gain a better chance of getting on in life. A mere one in 30 of all 16 year old pupils were at independent schools recognised as efficient in 1975; but about a third of students going to Oxford and Cambridge went to these schools, and about one in six of students going to all universities. In independent schools recognised as efficient, 31 per cent of the school leavers had passed three or more 'A' Levels in 1975, compared to 44.5 per cent in direct grant schools and 29.3 per cent in grammar schools.

The record of top public schools is more striking. Westminster is one of the nine schools singled out by the Clarendon Commission of 1861–4 as 'significant of the position that a few schools have gained in the public eye'. More than a hundred years later, the 'Clarendon' schools (Westminster, Eton, Harrow, Charterhouse, Merchant Taylors, Rugby, St Paul's, Shrewsbury and Winchester) are still important and prestigious. Tradition carries weight in public schools.

The younger Westminster boys (they start at 13) complain of a great emphasis on academic achievement and exam results. 'A lot of the masters press us. They expect a lot from us, far higher than a comprehensive standard.' Most of the boys take eight to ten 'O' Levels.

The Westminster sixth formers attribute the school's academic success to many causes. There is the atmosphere, 'the desire to learn', 'the relationship between master and pupil'. The teaching is stressed: 'The teachers are better, they have teachers that are not that qualified in state schools.' Parents exert pressure – 'We come from career-orientated families' – and in turn the pupils want to succeed: 'I work because of the thought of the advantages and opportunities it brings,' says John Holt who wants to be an archaeologist in America ('where the money is'). Fee-paying, in itself, is seen as bringing hard work and consequent success: 'By paying the money your parents are putting trust in you and you feel obliged to fulfil that trust.'

The Westminster boys go mainly into the traditional professions: law, medicine, accountancy, civil service – plus the media. The public schools, as a whole, retain a near-monopoly of the top jobs. The Clarendon schools, in particular, are still pervasive.

Anthony Giddens, The Cambridge sociologist, and Phil Stanworth, of York, found in their study of elites that, in 1970, 70 per cent of directors in the top 50 industrial firms were old boys of public schools (taken as the 200 or so Head Masters' Conference schools).

Almost a third of the financial directors of the largest merchant banks (the 18 or so clearing houses), the big four clearing banks, and the top eight or nine insurance companies in 1970 had been to Eton. Over four in five of these financial directors had been to Head Masters' Conference schools.

In the army, 86 per cent of the officers of the rank of major general and above had been to public schools in 1970 – an increase on earlier parts of the century. The air force leaders are drawn from a wider background: even so, two-thirds of the rank of vice marshall and above came from public schools in 1971.

In the legal profession, the old school tie rules. Over three-quarters of high court judges between 1960–9 went to public schools. Go up the legal ladder to principal judges, and the school selectivity increases: over four in five had been to public schools and four in ten to Clarendon schools.

The path to Whitehall corridors of power is still public schools and Oxbridge. In 1950, 59 per cent of under-secretaries and above were educated in public schools; by 1970 this figure had risen to 62 per cent. Between 1945 and 1963, three-quarters of permanent secretaries and the equivalent were educated at some sort of private school. Between 1971 and 1975, public school people made up over half the entrants, though under a quarter of the applicants.

Joanna Mack *Schools for Privilege* 1977

1 What reasons were given for the success that public schoolboys had in getting into top jobs?

2 Sociologists say that roles and statuses are 'achieved' when they are gained by someone's individual efforts. They are 'ascribed' when they are in some way handed down through the family or as a result of advantages of birth. To what extent does the success of public schoolboys depend on 'achievement' and 'ascription'?

3 Joanna Mack comments that 'independent schools remain controversial'. Why is this? What are the arguments for and against private education?

23

Learning to labour

Why do working class kids get working class jobs? Paul Willis' study of 'Learning to labour' tried to find out. In this extract Perc and his mates have been watching a careers film.

PERC: I wonder why there's never kids like us in films, see what our attitude is to work.

FUZZ: They're all ear'oles.

PERC: All goodygoodies.

WILL: No, you can tell they've been told what to say. They'm probably at some acting school or summat y'known, and they've got the opportunity to do this job – film careers for other kids. And you've gotta say this, wait for your cue, wait till he's finished his lines.

This is a group of boys commenting on careers films. They were at a single sex secondary modern school in a working class area. Perc, Fuzz and Will are 'lads'. The lads are the nonconformists in a school. Conformists are called 'ear'oles' or, more succinctly, 'lobes'. The division was at its clearest in this school because it was not masked by class, ability and sex differences.

Many studies of schools have indicated the same basic division of pupils. The 'disruptive minority' – i.e. the lads – has achieved a kind of notoriety after numerous reports of violence in the classroom and anxious statements from the teachers' unions. The raising of the school-leaving age in 1973, and the move towards large, difficult-to-police comprehensives, has increased the size, and certainly the stridency, of this counter-school culture. But what part do the rival conformist and nonconformist cultures really play in schools?

Compare the response of the 'ear'oles' to the careers films to that of the 'lads'. Tony and Nigel are 'ear'oles'.

TONY: Well, they opened your eyes, sort of. Being a milkman, get up at five o'clock in the morning, get up, get out, getting up in the dark.

NIGEL: The one on the post office, I thought it was good. They've helped people, the people who are interested in that particular line, you know, the job.

General advice on the best way to get a job and get on in it are also interpreted in polar ways. I asked Nigel about the way the careers teacher had handled things. The teacher had said: 'School's the same as work, and if you're not doing something at school, you're not going to do well at work. It's in your interests to do things at school, so that we can write them into the reports.' Nigel felt, 'He's doing it good. A lot of the time, you know, what he says is right.' But I also asked Spanksey, Joey and Fuzz:

SPANKSEY: After a bit you tek no notice of him. He says the same thing over and over again.

JOEY: We're always too busy fucking picking your nose, or flicking papers, we just don't listen to him.

FUZZ: He's always on about if you go for a job, you've got to do this, you've got to do that. Qualifications and everything. I've done it. You don't have to do none of that. Just go to a place, ask the man in charge. Nothing like what he says.

Both groups of boys readily transposed their present feelings onto their future, and also on to the future of those they contrasted with themselves. Joey and Spanksey speak for the 'lads':

JOEY: We wanna live for now, wanna live while we're young, want money to go out with, wanna go with women now, wanna have cars now, and er'm think about five, ten, fifteen years' time when it comes. But other people (like the 'ear'oles'), they'm getting their exams, they'm working, having no social life, having no fun, and they're waiting for fifteen years' time when they're people when they've got married and things like that. I think that's the difference. We are thinking about now, and having a laff now, and they're thinking about the future.

JOEY: I think they're the ones that have got the proper view of life (i.e. the 'ear'oles'). They're the ones that abide by the rules. They're the civil servant types. They'll have 'ouses and everything before us. They'll be the toffs. We'll be the brickies and things.

SPANKSEY: I think that we . . ., more or less, we're the ones that do the hard grafting but not they, they'll be the office workers. I ain't got no ambitions. I don't wanna have. I just want to have a nice wage, that'ud just see me through.

JOEY: I don't say it's wise. I say it's better for us. People the likes of us, we've tasted not the good life, you know – say, the social life what you'd have when you're older. I think we just like it too much. I know I do anyway. I don't think you can cut yourself off from it now and do an apprenticeship and all that . . . and not have much bread.

And Tony speaks for the 'lobes':

TONY: Well, I mean, it should be better for us, because we've had to face up to the fact that we've got to come to school. We've got to do the work, else you wouldn't get on. So you more or less train yourself to be like that. But I think the ones who haven't you know, which aren't bothered (i.e. the 'lads'), they'll go to work and they'll think, 'Ooh, I don't like this, I'll leave it.' Instead of sticking at it, they won't get on well in it.

The response of the conformist boys is not so surprising. They reflect what schooling is supposed to be about. The response of the nonconformist 'lads' is of more interest. It is not simply interesting because of its mere inversion of the conformist view, and its statement of the time-honoured notion of 'instant gratification'. The 'lads' response evokes an entire culture. They are speaking from the taken for-granted meanings at the heart of the counter-culture. This counter-culture forms their views about many things and – perhaps most important – their notion of what to expect in the future from a working life.

It is always difficult to generalise from small scale case study research. But I would suggest that these systematic differences amount to class differences between the 'respectable' and 'rough' working class. They also show how these classes reproduce themselves generation after generation.

At the present time, youth unemployment is the most pressing problem we have. Certainly it's better to have any kind of job than none at all. Concern with the present situation, however, should not obscure the basic processes I am pointing to. The form of people's relation to the productive process, and their own labour power, is of the utmost importance to all the situations in which they find themselves: at work, at home, on the streets or unemployed.

Paul Willis *Lads, Lobes and Labour* 1976

1 What is meant by the following terms?

a 'lobes' or 'ear'oles'
b 'lads'
c culture
d polar
e transposed
f conformist
g inversion
h instant gratification
i counter-culture

2 What did the 'lobes' and the 'lads' each think about the following:

a school
b careers lessons
c work
d the future
e 'lobes'
f 'lads'?

3 What does Willis suggest is the basis for these two cultures – the school culture, and its opposite – the counter-culture?

4 Discuss in your class what you think Willis means when he writes: 'they show how these classes *reproduce* themselves'.

'Good. We're middle class!'

24

Marx and Engels on class

Karl Marx and his friend Friedrich Engels published the *Communist Manifesto* in 1848. The bourgeoisie can roughly be thought of as the middle class and the proletariat as the working class.

The history of all hitherto existing society is the history of class struggles.

Freeman and slave, patrician and plebeian, lord and serf, guild master and journeyman, in a word, oppressor and oppressed, stood in constant opposition to one another, carried on an uninterrupted, now hidden, now open fight, a fight that each time ended either in a revolutionary reconstitution of society at large or in the common ruin of the contending classes.

In the earlier epochs of history we find almost everywhere a complicated arrangement of society into various orders, a manifold gradation of social rank. In ancient Rome we have patricians, knights, plebeians, slaves; in the middle ages, feudal lords, vassals, guild masters, journeymen, apprentices, serfs; in almost all of these classes, again, subordinate gradations.

The modern bourgeois society that has sprouted from the ruins of feudal society has not done away with class antagonisms. It has but established new classes, new conditions of oppression, new forms of struggle in place of the old ones.

Our epoch, the epoch of the bourgeoisie, possesses, however, this distinctive feature: it has simplified the class antagonisms. Society as a whole is more and more splitting up into two great hostile camps, into two great classes directly facing each other: bourgeoisie and proletariat.

Karl Marx and Friedrich Engels *The Communist Manifesto* 1959

1 Marx believed that history followed a pattern and that particular relationships would keep reappearing. Draw two columns. Head one column 'Oppressors' and the other 'Oppressed'. List the various groups who had been oppressors or oppressed at various times in the past.

2 Why did Marx believe that our epoch, or age, has simplified class antagonisms?

3 Marx and Engels wrote this as a 'manifesto'. Find out what a manifesto is and suggest why Marx chose to write it in this way.

25

Caste

William and Charlotte Wiser lived in the Indian village of Karimpur. They describe the caste system that they found there.

The leaders of our village are so sure of their power that they make no effort to display it. The casual visitor finds little to distinguish them from other farmers. They dress as simply and cheaply as their neighbours, and do no more shouting or scolding; they work as faithfully as any in their fields; the walls enclosing their family courtyards may be high but are no better kept than those adjoining them, and their entrances are often less elaborate. And yet when one of them appears among men of serving caste, the latter express respect and fear in every guarded word and gesture. The serving ones have learned that as long as their subservience is unquestioned, the hand which directs them rests lightly. But let there be any move toward independence or even indifference among them, and the paternal touch becomes a stranglehold.

In our village the economic power of the leaders is strengthened by their religious and social influence as Brahmans. The right of Brahmans to dictate may be challenged in the cities, but in villages like ours their control is absolute. Their birth as Brahmans is evidence of their superiority. Many an important decision in a humble section of the village waits on their divinely guided sanction. Although they occupy themselves as farmers and grain lenders, two or three of them are called upon to officiate as priests in ceremonies of grave importance to villagers. As with their economic power, they find it unnecessary to proclaim their authority as Brahmans. But if anyone fails to recognise the existence of this authority, he is reminded of it so effectively that he does not err again.

Between these Brahmans and the next group of farmers lie the two great divisions, *kshatriya* and *vaisya*, including many castes, pictured as the arms and body supporting the Brahman head. These divisions are represented by only a few families in Karimpur. Below them are the *sudras*, the feet. Chief in number and importance among *sudras* in our village are the *kachhis*, farmers who work on land which they rent for their own use or which they rent on shares with Brahmans. They have been brought up, like their forefathers, with the assurance that their mission in life is to till the soil and to accept the will of their superiors. They live in a little colony of joint family enclosures apart from the rest of the village. As soon as one of their boys can lift a head load of grain or drive a bullock, he is expected to help. From then on he carries his full share until old age entitles him to partial rest. Severe illness may grant him a respite, but as soon as he can move, he must resume his duties.

In addition to the *kachhis* there are eleven castes in Karimpur counted as *sudras*. None are as self-sufficient as the *kachhis* who have before them the hope that they or their sons may some day pay off their heavy debts to village leaders. The other *sudras* accept indebtedness and obligations to *jajmans* (patrons) as the order of life. When we first came to Karimpur we regarded the carpenters (one of the *sudra* castes) as independent craftsmen. They work in the lane that runs in front of their row of houses, making and repairing the carts, ploughs, and other implements of the farmers. Later as we stood watching their work, we overheard patrons ordering – not asking – them to make new handles for tools or to complete some house repairs. We realised that they were not independent, as we had thought. To get their payment, which for carpenters is fixed, they must go daily to the fields of their patrons during the harvest season to receive their share of the crop. The shares are given out more as donations than as payments due, and place upon the recipient an obligation which he can never quite repay.

Still lower than the *sudras* in the Karimpur social scale are the untouchables. Although barred from the four great divisions which include all of the accepted castes – the *brahmans*, *kshatriyas*, *vaisyas*, and *sudras* – they have a carefully graduated caste system of their own. A leather worker and a sweeper are both untouchables. And the leather worker would not degrade himself by eating or drinking with the sweeper, nor would he consider marrying his daughter to the sweeper's son. Highest among the untouchable of Karimpur is the *dhobi*, whose appointed task is to wash the skirts and scarves, the shirts and loin cloths of the villagers.

His position in the village is more like that of a *sudra*. But he is an untouchable, according to the traditional law. The rock on which he beats the villagers' garments is at the edge of the pond beside our grove. He washes the clothes of high caste families regularly. Housewives of lower castes complain that he often neglects their washing, if not reminded. The lowest of the untouchables must keep their own garments clean. He refuses to touch them.

William and Charlotte Wiser *Behind Mud Walls* 1963

1 Which are the four main castes in Hindu society?

2 Which other group is outside of the four main castes?

3 Each caste is divided into many subcastes, or jatis. How many subcastes are there in the *sudras* caste in Karimpur? Name two of them and say how they earn their livelihood.

4 The castes are sometimes compared to the parts of the body. Which castes are which parts of the body?

5 The Hindu caste system has four main features:
a it is based on occupation, or jobs;
b it is closely tied to religion and the idea of 'ritual purity' (keeping yourself clean and free from defilement by contact with lower castes);
c it is endogamous (individuals must marry within their caste);
d it is hereditary (people are born into castes and remain in that caste throughout their lives).
Find examples of each of these features in the extract.

6 How does caste differ from other forms of stratification such as class or estate.

26
Class
divisions

Robert Roberts writes about life in Salford in the first quarter of the twentieth century. His mother and father owned a grocery shop in a poor area of the city and it was here that Robert grew up.

To the outsider the people who lived in the district were just 'poor', or 'low class'. To the people themselves there were clear divisions within the community, based on differences of status. Very few people had much wealth and they had very little power to influence their lives. Each family's position was marked by the way they behaved, dressed and spent what little money they had.

In our community, as in every other of its kind, each street had the usual social rating; one side or one end of that street might be classed higher than another. Weekly rents varied from 2s 6d for the back-to-back to 4s 6d for a 'two up and two down'. End houses often had special status. Every family, too, had a ranking, and even individual members within it; neighbours would consider a daughter in one household as 'dead common' while registering her sister as 'refined', a word much in vogue. Class divisions were of the greatest consequence, though their implications remained unrealised: the many looked upon social and economic inequality as the law of nature. Division in our own society ranged from an élite at the peak, composed of the leading families, through recognised strata to a social base whose members one damned as the 'lowest of the low', or simply 'no class'. Shopkeepers, publicans and skilled tradesmen occupied the premier positions, each family having its own sphere of influence. A few of these aristocrats, while sharing working class culture, had aspirations. From their ranks the lower middle class, then clearly defined, drew most of its recruits – clerks and, in particular, schoolteachers (struggling hard at that time for social position). Well before translation those striving to 'get on' tried to ape what they believed were 'real' middle class manners and customs. Publicans' and shopkeepers' daughters, for instance set the fashion in clothes for a district. Some went to private commercial colleges in the city, took music lessons or perhaps studied elocution – that short cut, it was felt, to 'culture' – at two shillings an hour, their new 'twang' tried out later over the bar and counter, earning them a deal of covert ridicule. Top families generally stood ever on the lookout for any activity or 'nice' connection which might edge them, or at least their children, into a higher social ambience. But despite all endeavour, mobility between manual workers, small tradesmen and the genuine middle class remained slight, and no one needed to wonder why; before the masses rose an economic barrier that few men could ever hope to scale. At the end of the Edwardian period an adult male industrial worker earned £75 a year; the average annual salary of a man in the middle classes proper was £340.

That wide section beyond the purely manual castes where incomes ranged between the two norms mentioned was considered by many to be no more than 'jumped up working class', not to be confused with the true order above: but the striving sought it nevertheless, if not for themselves, at least for their children. The real social divide existed between those who, in earning daily bread, dirtied hands and face and those who did not.

The less ambitious among skilled workers had aims that seldom rose above saving enough to buy the ingoing of a beer-house, open a corner shop or get a boarding house at the seaside. By entering into any business at all a man and his family grew at once in economic status, though social prestige accrued much more slowly. Fiascos were common; again and again one noticed in the district pathetic attempts to set up shops in private houses by people who possessed only a few shillings' capital and no experience. After perhaps only three weeks one saw their hopes collapse, often to the secret satisfaction of certain neighbours who, in the phrase of the times, 'hated to see folk trying to get on'.

On the social ladder after tradesmen and artisans came the semi-skilled workers (still a small section) in regular employment, and then the various grades of unskilled labourers. These divisions could be marked in many public houses, where workers other than craftsmen would be frozen or flatly ordered out of those rooms in which journeymen forgathered. Each part of the tavern had its status rating; indeed, 'he's only a tap room man' stood as a common slur.

Robert Roberts *The Classic Slum* 1971

1 What do you understand by the following terms?

a social class   e status
b elite   f aspirations
c aristocrat   g salary
d social mobility h strata

2 Which occupations had the highest status in the community?

3 How was their influence felt by other groups within the area?

4 How easy was it for members of the working class to 'get on' and enter the middle class?

5 What was the 'real social divide'?

6 Class divisions are based on a combination of economic factors (income and wealth), social factors (status and prestige), and political factors (power and the ability to choose). Find examples in the passage for each of these aspects of stratification.

7 American anthropologist Oscar Lewis has claimed that there is a 'culture of poverty', a set of attitudes and values, which separates the slum dweller from the 'culture' of the wider society outside of the slum. What evidence is there in Robert Roberts' description of Salford which either supports or disproves this point of view.

" *Yes, I'm on Social Security . . . No, I've never done a hand's turn in my life . . . Yes, I'm of Irish extraction . . .*"

27

The class barrier

Social mobility means the movement of individuals and families from one social class to another. But is there a barrier between blue collar (or manual worker) classes and white collar (or non-manual) classes? Anthony Heath considers the evidence from the Oxford Mobility Enquiry.

There is no barrier in any literal sense. If we say the classes I, II and III are those above the barrier, it is clear that about a quarter of the men from working class social origins succeeded in crossing this barrier. And the men who got across it did not collapse, exhausted from the effort, on the ground immediately beyond the barrier. Having crossed it, the working class man was just as likely to carry on all the way into the higher grade professional, administrative or managerial jobs of class I as he was to end up in the routine clerical work of class III.

True, rather fewer men from class I were likely to cross the barrier in the other direction into the working class. This has led writers like Blau and Duncan to talk of a 'semi-permeable membrane' or 'one way screen' which it is easier to pass through in one direction than the other. They went on to say: 'Some white collar occupations require much less skill and command considerably less income than many blue collar occupations. This makes it possible for men with inferior abilities who want to remain in the white collar classes to do so. The existence of relatively unskilled white collar occupations, such as retail sales and clerical jobs, makes it possible for the unsuccessful sons of white collar workers to remain in the white collar class by paying the price of accepting a lower income than they might have been able to obtain in a manual occupation. This is in many ways a plausible argument, but let us look at the actual evidence for Britain. Let us compare the occupations entered by 'unsuccessful' men with inferior abilities from different social origins. For the present purposes we can define the unsuccessful as those who went to elementary or secondary modern schools and left at the minimum school-leaving age without any formal academic qualifications such as school certificate or 'O' Level. The question we now have to ask is whether these unsuccessful men from white collar homes were largely absorbed by unskilled white collar jobs like retail sales and routine clerical work.

The short answer for Britain is a firm 'No'. Some of these men (rather surprisingly perhaps) managed to get class I and II jobs, but even if we put all the white collar occupations together, they still absorbed only 24 per cent of these unqualified offspring of white collar fathers. This is a bit better than the unqualified children of blue collar workers managed – 15 per cent got into these jobs – but it is hardly adequate evidence for a boundary that 'creates relative protection against the danger of downward mobility from the white collar to the blue collar class'. The great majority of educationally unsuccessful men with 'inferior abilities' seem to end up in some kind of blue collar work.

But did they jump or were they pushed? Did these educationally unsuccessful men enter blue collar work because they were excluded from the white collar work they would have liked, or did they actually choose manual work for its higher pay despite the absence of 'the cherished symbol of the white collar'? The answer may tell us some thing about the prevalence of status snobbery in Britain, a snobbery that is often asserted by commentators on British life but rarely demonstrated.

The lesson is simple. Qualifications improve your chances of getting a better paid job (although they do not ensure it). If you miss out on the qualifications to be won at school, try for the vocational ones that can be obtained after leaving school. White collar families tend to know this lesson; they are better at securing school credentials in the first place, and they seem better at using the 'alternative route' of technical and vocational qualifications if they miss out first time around. There is little sign that they allow snobbery to stand in the way of economic self-interest. It is a good bet that many of these 'downwardly mobile' men jumped into skilled manual work for the better pay and prospects which, compared with the alternatives, it offered them.

Table 2 The destinations of 'educationally unsuccessful men'

Father's class	Non-manual			Manual				Total
	I	II	III	IV	V	VI	VIII	
	%	%	%	%	%	%	%	
Non-manual (I–III)	7.8	7.4	8.8	9.8	14.5	23.6	28.3	100.2
Manual (V–VII)	3.4	5.4	6.6	7.4	13.0	30.4	33.8	100

Respondent's class in 1972

Anthony Heath *Social Mobility* 1981

1 From the evidence in the table calculate the percentage of educationally unsuccessful men whose fathers were in manual occupations who crossed 'the barrier' in 1972?

2 Using the same table calculate the number of educationally unsuccessful men who crossed in the other direction into manual work in 1972.

3 What proportion of all men of working class social origins crossed the barrier?

4 Which is more likely:
a men from classes IV to VIII crossing into non-manual jobs or
b men from classes I to III crossing into manual work? How do Blau and Duncan explain this trend?

5 Does Anthony Heath's evidence support this view? Explain your answer.

6 How do the children of white collar workers gain the advantage whether they do well at school or not?

28

Women in pubs

The American sociologist Erving Goffman writes of social life taking place in 'settings' which form a kind of stage for the action that takes place. A school classroom, for example, is easily recognised as a different kind of setting from a law court or a hospital because of the different props it contains.

The nature of the setting tells us something about what goes on within them. People make 'fronts' which tell others what they want them to know. Doctors wear white coats, judges wear wigs, pupils wear uniform. Anne Garvey writes about a pub as a particular setting in which men and women create different 'fronts'.

There's something very tricky about being a woman alone in a pub, even if you do stick to the lounge part and have a bitter lemon. You are in foreign territory and although you know there are going to be no open hostilities, you are expected to go through the motions of defensive action to acknowledge the presence of the native inhabitants. It doesn't really matter how you do it, although a newspaper can look a bit assertive and most women settle for a cover behind a book, or a magazine or even a railway timetable – anything, as long as you're not just brazenly looking around.

Men go to pubs for a variety of reasons. They may want to be alone, to lean on the bar and sup their beer silently, observing the scene. Or they may go for company, to meet a friend or just to talk informally and anonymously to people they've never met before. The pub is a preserve. It has its own conventions. A certain method of address and precedent operates – special behaviour applies.

Women have been admitted as guests for some time. It's not their business to sort out the collective finances of a night out. They're not required to jostle round the bar or exchange jokes with the landlord. They are accompanied, escorted, officially approved by their association with a recognised companion. Their role is to sit and wait quietly if their men want to have a laugh with the boys en route for the bar, or smile resignedly if the lads play darts.

Women on their own are intruders in this highly evolved man-to-man encounter. They're made to feel miserable, out of place and unwelcome. The best they can do is to seem to be waiting for someone: sitting back and relaxing would be a gesture of insolent provocation.

Ask any woman what's the major hazard of single pub going. It's the imminent fear of a pick up – the 'We know what you're really up to' bit. I think we can all explain how the association between pubs and sex grew up. There was the squalor of Victorian parlours with the pub being the traditional haunt of prostitutes. Yet the transition into both respectability and equality is more difficult in publand: the landscape is hostile to the traditional feminine values of domesticity. A pub is another world, it's not meant to be like home. It's the other part of a man's life and he has never wanted any reminder of the little woman waiting at home to enter this escape world.

The bare tables and the beermats exist to enshrine that central symbol, the pint. Beer has developed as a man's drink. It takes some getting through and long practice. Women who plunge in and order a pint give a reckless, if unconscious challenge to the man's right. Pints are for quaffing. You open the back of your throat and pour it down. You've got to have a 'good clack' as they say in Yorkshire. In the North especially, beer is marketed as a man's drink. Steel-eyed muscled types lounge aggressively across publicity posters. Grimy but bronzed workmen stride assertively across television set bar-rooms. Women have never been initiated into the mysteries of this male camaraderie. They either stick to sipping or they just settle for a half pint. Women are the intruders who connive at their own exclusion. They threaten the spontaneity and the open-mindedness of masculine society. 'Whenever a woman gets out her purse to pay,' a male friend remarked to me the other day. 'It's a major operation. I always feel it's the housekeeping she's spending.'

It probably is. The easy flow of cash from a man's back pocket is the gesture of generations of financial dominance. It's cash to do what he likes with: he worked for it after all. A woman's enforced caution tends to compulsively translate six pints and two gin and tonics into new socks for the children, or a wall can opener. But in many working class pubs there's a special bar for ladies: remember Ena, Martha and Minnie Caldwell in the Snug? Friday night out with the girls is today commonplace everywhere. These mass giggle-ins are deceptive steps in the acceptance of women. They're not really related to the pub question. The women go along together. They stick seated in a large homogenous hilarious group and bother no one.

Anne Garvey *New Society* 1974

1 What makes a pub a predominantly masculine 'setting'? Make a list of the 'props' which, according to Anne Garvey, serve to keep women in their place.

2 Woman who go into pubs may either go in alone, with a man, or with other women. What is the appropriate behaviour described for each of these situations?

3 Describe the different 'fronts' used by men and women in pubs.

4 Make a collection of advertisements for different drinks – beer, spirits, wines etc. What can you tell from the adverts about the social setting into which those drinks might fit?

29
Man in the street

What do we see when we observe someone standing on a street corner? What are the messages we pick up? How do we interpret them? What meanings do they have for us? How are those meanings influenced by the colour of the person's skin? Ann Dummett describes how six different people 'see' a man standing on the corner of the street.

Standing on the corner of the street is a man. Broad-shouldered, five foot ten in smart new shoes, he is dressed for a summer day: pink shirt, polished cotton trousers from a multiple store, and a thick knitted jacket with bone buttons. There's a pub on the corner: an old brown English town pub, with clouded windows marked in whirligig lettering; the brickwork, streaked in grime, has weathered into its undistinguished surroundings. Next door, a row of brick terrace houses runs for fifty yards towards a brash new furniture store, blazoning its mottled carpets and expensive three-piece suites across a plate glass window. Two children are playing hopscotch. Across the road, a Peugeot pulls up at the small filling station incongruously stuck between more houses, whose milkbottles, on every step, proclaim them occupied.

The man is waiting for someone. People pass by him every few seconds, for the corner is at one end of a shopping street, where Tesco's, Radio Rentals, Mr Flaherty's Bargain Shop (washing machines and radios!!) and Marjorie's Hairdressing of Paris offer a consumer's paradise for the not-so-rich. To everyone who passes, he is someone different. Many fail to notice him at all. A few register his presence as a black man, hanging round a street corner. A middle aged lady of straitened means, going by neatly and gloved to Tesco's where the meat is cheaper, pays him a longer glance with a romantic eye. How beautiful the pink shirt looks against the brown, blue-shadowed skin. Like the Gauguin reproductions she learnt to admire in her youth. To her, the romance of the noble savage illuminates this prosaic and completely unsavage individual. But something about him – the knitted jacket, perhaps – does not quite fit the aloof dignity a brown man should, in her view, possess. She passes on to the supermarket – where the Jamaican girl on the checking-out desk (who happens to be the cousin of the man on the corner) arouses in her no thought of Gauguin or noble savagery at all. She is just another cashier in an overall, ringing up the lowest grocery bill in town.

Two blond youths, eighteen and nineteen, builder's labourers, walk past the man next. He's a blackie to them, the sort who always whines when he's given the heavy jobs. They had one of his sort on the last site they worked on. They called him Sambo. Sullen, he was. Complained to the foreman that he was always left to lift pipes, when they were up on the scaffolding. They fixed him. They put Bill's wallet into his donkey jacket pocket. That got him fired. The foreman had been fed up with him anyway. They're all the same, think they own the bloody country.

The Peugeot has driven away from the filling station, and a Triumph Herald draws up. The driver, a girl in sunglasses, pulls in to fill up before zooming down the motorway to tea in rural Berkshire. She hasn't long to get to the shadowed drawing room, twenty miles and a generation away, where the view through the window is across a soft lawn to the quiet and expensive Thames. She sees the man on the corner, and watches him idly as the filling station attendant attends to the petrol. Why, she wonders, do all coloured people hang round the street corners? She has nothing against coloured people. Actually, of course, she doesn't know any, except a few like that Dr Ram she met at some awful garden fête, but of course he wasn't like a coloured person really; he was educated, which is different. Incurious, and seeing nothing in the man across the road, she drives away, her mind tightly closed to the world around her, encased in the steel and glass of the car, passing unaffected through the shopping crowds.

The next passerby, an elderly lady dressed in the kind of fashion the *Daily Telegraph* Women's page was advocating ten years ago, sees the man on the corner and, rather uncertainly, smiles at him in case he is Nigerian. Her elder brother, Robert, whom she has adored since childhood, spent years in Nigeria; he loved the people there and they simply adored him, of course. She is not *quite* sure that this man could possibly be Nigerian, because his clothes don't look quite right; all the same, she never misses a chance to make one of them feel at home in England, for Robert's sake. Poor dears, they must feel so cold when they come here.

'Hullo Bert!' calls an English bus conductor, walking past the corner to reach the bus garage. 'Hullo there,' answers the man on the corner. So his name is Bert. As matter of fact, his full name is Horatio Herbert Fraser, but his English mates call him Bert. He is a bus conductor, now off duty and waiting to meet his wife so that they can go shopping together. The friend who has just hailed him in a cheery way is Fred Walton, who lives a few doors away from him. Fred, walking past the corner of the street, has recognised in him not an anonymous 'coloured man', but one of his mates.

Ann Dummett *A Portrait of English Racism* 1973

1 The way we see people is often summed up in the words and phrases we use to describe them. To the middle aged lady Horatio Herbert Fraser was a 'noble savage'. How did the other people describe him?

2 Ideas about people or groups which are contained in a single word or phrase are called 'stereotypes'. Very often the imagined characteristics of a group of people are applied to each individual who belongs to that group. This extract is full of stereotypes. In your own words describe the stereotypes of the following groups of people:
a 'middle aged ladies of straitened means'
b 'coloured people'
c 'Triumph Herald drivers from rural Berkshire'
d 'builder's labourers'

3 Many stereotypes can be described as 'racist' because they are based on the view that differences between people are the result of hereditary differences within different racial groups. In what ways might the following statements be described as racist?
a 'he wasn't like a coloured person really, he was educated'
b 'Poor dears, they must feel so cold when they come here.'
c 'something about him – the knitted jacket, perhaps – does not fit the aloof dignity a brown man, in her view, should possess'
d 'a blackie, the sort that always whines when he's given the heavy jobs'.

30
Migration

There is nothing new about migration. From the very earliest times people have moved about from place to place across the face of the Earth. Everyone's ancestors, at some time in the past, have been migrants. Immigration into Britain since the 1950s is only a further stage in that long history of migration. The 1967 PEP survey used a sample of 3,292 people, whose families came from the Caribbean, India, Pakistan or Bangladesh, to study the facts of racial disadvantage.

There is now a population of about 750,000 adults from racial minority groups in England and Wales. Nearly all these people are immigrants (less than 2 per cent were born in Britain) and nearly all have come here over the past 20 years (only 8 per cent of Asians and West Indians said that they came to Britain before 1956). This represents a very substantial wave of migration of people from developing countries which have historical ties with Britain into England's towns and urban centres. This migration can be likened to the movement of agricultural workers in nineteenth century England to the towns, where they came to form the new working class. The treatment of the working class by the middle class in Victorian times was similar to the treatment of Asians and West Indians by whites in the 1960s.

Another, more topical, parallel can be drawn from the present movement of people from the countryside to the towns within all developing countries. Extreme poverty and lack of work cause people to move, for example, from the Peruvian countryside into Lima, or from the Indian countryside into Calcutta – so that the population of such towns has multiplied rapidly over the past 20 years (the same period as the migration to Britain). Migrating to Britain may be seen as an alternative to migrating to the towns within the home country, which are not able to provide enough employment for those arriving from the countryside. The advantage of coming to Britain is that there is a much better prospect of work; the 1967 PEP study showed that while 59 per cent of Pakistanis had been unemployed immediately before coming to Britain, only about 6 per cent were unemployed here (a level of unemployment which was nevertheless twice the national average). There are also the attractions of a higher standard of living, better education and social security. The disadvantage of coming here (compared with moving to the town within the home country) is that it means becoming a member of a small minority within an alien culture. A move from the countryside to the town within the home country must make great demands on people's powers of adaptation; but the contrast between life in an Indian or Pakistani village and life in an industrial town in the North of England is so great in every way that the people who decide to make such a move must do so out of urgent need.

The reasons for migrating can be divided into factors leading people to want to change their way of life (the push) and factors attracting them to go to live in a particular country as the solution to their problem (the pull). It is plain that lack of work is the worst problem shared by the largest number of people, and this must be what produces most of the push towards migration. A study carried out by Peach in the

73

1960s suggested that employment was also a major factor attracting people to England. If the level of Commonwealth immigration was plotted against the level of job vacancies in England a strong relationship was found: when job vacancies went up immigration also went up, after a time lag, and when vacancies went down, immigration went down. It seems therefore that work has provided both the push and the pull for the migration. This conclusion is fully supported by the findings of the survey. Towards the beginning of the interview informants who were aged 15 or more when they came to this country were asked: 'Why did you come to Britain?'

Over half of the men (57 per cent) say that they came to Britain to get work or to earn money, and this is much the most frequently mentioned reason for coming. Although the men tended to be pioneers in the migration, there is an important minority of them (16 per cent) who came to join their families. The other main reasons given by men for migrating are to seek a better future or life for the family (17 per cent) – which may be a rather more idealistic way of expressing the need for work – and education (13 per cent). An important minority also moved for political reasons (8 per cent). Over two-thirds of women say that they came to Britain to join their husbands or for other family reasons; in general, therefore, it was the men who pioneered the migration, while the women followed on later.

David J. Smith *The Facts of Racial Disadvantage* 1976

1 People migrate because of 'push' and 'pull' influences. Make a list of factors which might:
a 'push' people to migrate;
b 'pull' people to migrate.

2 Migration takes place both within a country and between different countries. Give three examples of migration within a country.

3 Why would those who migrate between countries very often only 'do so out of urgent need'?

4 Many of the African Asians who were included in the survey were forced to leave Uganda by the then ruler, Idi Amin. They were often businessmen and shopowners who had been settled in Uganda for many years. How might the reasons for their migration have influenced the answers they gave to the PEP survey?

Table 3   Why did you come to Britain?
Men aged 15 and over at migration

| Percentage of men who mentioned | | Men by country of origin: | | | |
	All men	West Indians	Pakistanis/ Bangladeshis	Indians	African Asians
	%	%	%	%	%
Jobs/opportunities/ money	57	53	89	64	26
To join family etc.	16	11	10	21	17
Better future or life	17	24	13	15	10
Politics in home country	8	1	1	2	44
Education	13	9	13	18	20

(Some mentioned more than one reason.)

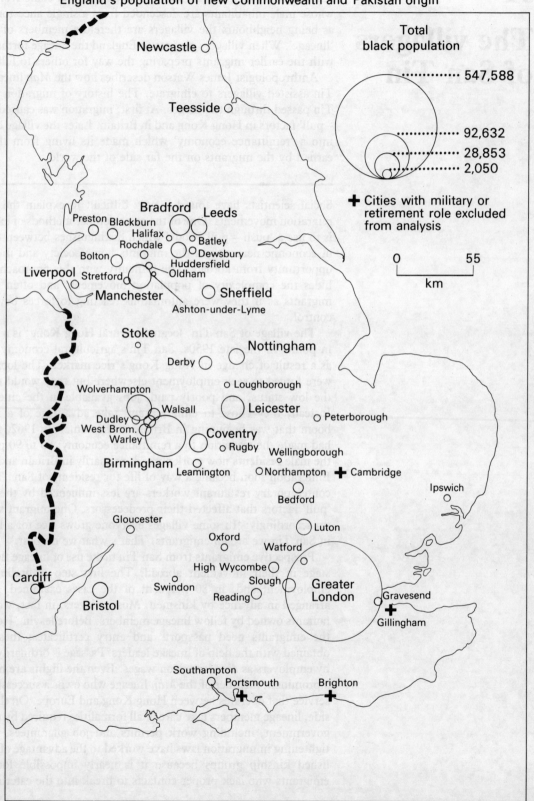

England's population of new Commonwealth and Pakistan origin

Total
black population

547,588

92,632

28,853

2,050

✚ Cities with military or
retirement role excluded
from analysis

0   55
└────────────┘
km

Newcastle

Teesside

Bradford
Leeds
Preston   Blackburn
          Halifax   Batley
          Rochdale   Dewsbury
Bolton   Huddersfield
Liverpool Stretford   Oldham
       Manchester   Sheffield
           Ashton-under-Lyme

Stoke

Nottingham
Derby

Loughborough
Wolverhampton
Walsall   Leicester
Dudley   Peterborough
West Brom.
Warley   Coventry
              Rugby
Birmingham   Wellingborough
       Leamington Northampton ✚ Cambridge
                                          Ipswich
                   Bedford
Gloucester
              Oxford   Luton
                     Watford
Cardiff   High Wycombe
        Swindon   Slough   Greater
          Reading   London
Bristol   ✚ Gravesend
                              Gillingham

Southampton
    Portsmouth   Brighton
        ✚   ✚

31

The villagers of San Tin

Many of the Chinese who come to live in Britain come from villages whose male inhabitants are descended from a single ancestor. As well as being neighbours the villagers are therefore members of the same 'lineage'. When villagers migrate to England the lineage forms a 'chain' with the earlier migrants preparing the way for others to follow.

Anthropologist James Watson describes how the *Man* lineage of San Tin assisted villagers to emigrate. The history of migration from San Tin passed through two stages. At first, migration was caused by 'push – pull' factors in Hong Kong and in Britain. Later the village developed into a 'remittance economy' which made its living from the money earned by the migrants on the far side of the world.

Social scientists have found it very difficult to explain the causes of migration movements. One of the most popular methods of explanation is to use a 'push – pull' model which distinguishes between the 'push' of economic necessity in the migrants home society and the 'pull' of opportunity from abroad. The difficulty with this approach is that it hides the complexity of population movements and often treats the migrants as if they were automatons reacting to forces beyond their control.

The village of San Tin, located in rural Hong Kong, is a good case in point. In the late 1950s, San Tin's agricultural economy collapsed as a result of change in Hong Kong's rice market. The local farmers were forced to seek employment elsewhere but they would not accept the low status, and poorly paid, jobs available in the cities nearby. Instead, they chose to emigrate and take advantage of a restaurant boom that was beginning in Britain at that time. By 1962, the village had made the transition to a remittance economy; 85 to 90 per cent of the male residents now work abroad, primarily in Britain and Holland. Emigration soon became a way of life for residents of San Tin and the contemporary restaurant workers are less influenced by the 'push' or 'pull' factors that affected their predecessors. One migrant summed it up accordingly: 'In some villages everyone grows rice for a living, but in San Tin we are all emigrants. That's what we do best.'

Prospective emigrants from San Tin make use of lineage ties at every stage in their movement abroad. The first step is finding suitable employment and, in 80 per cent of the cases examined, jobs were arranged in advance by kinsmen. Most villagers, in fact, work in restaurants owned by fellow lineage members. Before leaving Hong Kong, the emigrants need passports and entry certificates; these too are obtained with the help of lineage leaders. Passage is ordinarily provided by employers as an advance on wages. Even the flights are handled by a prominent member of the *Man* lineage who owns a successful charter service that operates between Hong Kong and Europe. On the London side, lineage members take care of all formalities required by the British government, including work permits and job guarantees. The ever-tightening immigration laws have worked to the advantage of the established kinship groups because it is nearly impossible for the new emigrants who lack proper contacts to break into the catering trade.

Emigration has strengthened the *Man* lineage as a social institution and made individual members even more dependent on their kinsmen than they may have been in the past. The lineage is so well suited to the requirements of chain migration that it has been converted into a kind of 'emigration agency'. It should be noted, however, that the *Man* lineage is an exceptional case; most of the Chinese in Britain are organised along different lines. Among the majority, the critical links in the chain are formed by members of an extended family – usually sets of brothers and their sons. As might be expected, the closed nature of the migration chains has important implications for the character of the Chinese community in Britain.

James Watson *Between Two Cultures* 1977

1 In your own words describe what is meant by the following terms?
a 'push – pull'
b remittance economy
c lineage
d chain migration
e extended family

2 How has migration strengthened the '*Man* lineage as a social institution'?

3 The Chinese in Britain form a closer knit community than many other immigrant groups. How has the pattern of Chinese migration made this possible?

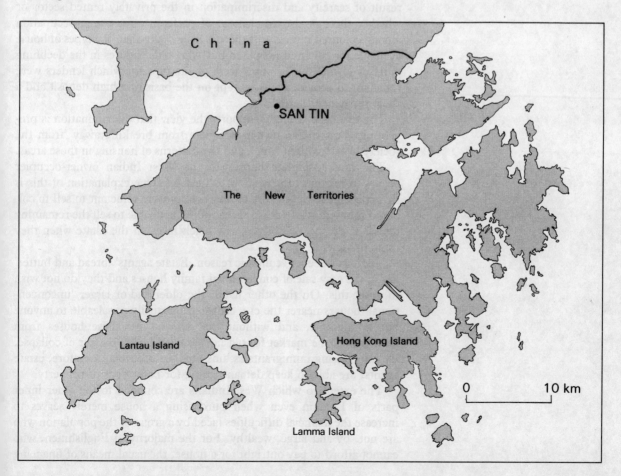

32

Discrimination in housing

Discrimination on the basis of ethnic background or skin colour is widespread in British society. In finding somewhere to live West Indian and Asians often find that they are trapped in districts on the edges of city centres where the houses are large and old. Such areas have been called 'zones of transition' (or twilight zones), because they were places to which immigrant groups came before moving out to more desirable districts further out of the city. For many West Indians in Britain it is very difficult to move out. In the communities which have developed in the 'zone of transition' it is common to find a number of families sharing a large house owned by one of them. The basis of this owner-occupied, multi-occupied housing is both social and economic. R. Haddon considers the key role of the estate agent in creating and maintaining this situation.

In looking for a house to purchase the crucial 'gatekeeper' steering the West Indian to 'suitable areas' is the estate agent. The estate agent is the central figure in the West Indian's search for a home, and one who is likely to practise discrimination, either on his own behalf, or because of alleged pressures from vendors and their neighbours. Whether the West Indian has been projected into owner-occupation primarily as a result of scarcity and discrimination in the privately rented sector or whether there is also an element of preference for owner-occupation among coloured immigrants there is little doubt that 'the types of house available for coloured people to buy were older houses in the declining parts of towns. Such houses were of the type for which lenders were reluctant to provide loans, except on the basis of a high deposit and a short repayment period.'

The evidence strongly supports the view that discrimination is preventing West Indian owner-occupiers from breaking away 'from the society of the twilight zone', and the patterns of housing in those areas.

The most complete barrier to the West Indian owner-occupier occurs in relation to new suburban estates. One explanation of this is that speculative developers of new estates were reluctant to sell to coloured immigrants, because of fear of being unable to sell the remaining houses if prospective buyers saw black faces on the estate when they came to view.

There is a deeper economic reason. Estate agents' 'bread and butter' lies in the easy sale of conventional family houses and they do not wish to upset this. On the other hand, the older and/or larger 'unconventional' houses nearer the city centre are virtually unsaleable to anyone but immigrants, and without the demand for these houses from immigrants, the market for old houses would be in danger of collapse. By categorising immigrants as 'unsuited' to suburbia, therefore, estate agents, are able to keep demand going for both types of property.

The extent to which West Indians are confined to the older inner parts of London even when purchasing a house merely serves to increase the financial difficulties faced by a group of the population who are not, by and large, wealthy. For the majority of Englishmen, who cannot afford to pay outright for a house, the usual means of financing is through a building society mortgage, or if this is not possible, through a mortgage from the local authority. It is the vast expansion of the building societies since the nineteenth century which has played an important part in shaping the trend towards owner-occupation in the English housing market, to such an extent that home ownership is now within the reach of at least a proportion of the working class. This, then, has become a major avenue for improving one's housing situation.

Regardless of the type of property and income resources of West Indians, Daniels found considerable discrimination with regard to the availability of building society mortgages to West Indians. This expresses itself in refusal to give mortgages, or the granting of mortgages only on stiffer terms (higher initial deposits, shorter repayment periods) and the frequency with which West Indians have made use of local authority mortgages, which are usually not available unless the applicant has been unable to obtain a commercial mortgage. Daniels suggests that although the reputable building societies claim only to apply universal criteria of eligibility for a mortgage, there is a danger that coloured applicants as a group are rated as unreliable. Again the estate agent appears as a critical figure, advising and selecting potential mortgage applicants. Leaving discrimination on the basis of colour aside, however, the West Indian is still at a disadvantage. Building societies are reluctant to lend on old property, the value of which may not represent sufficient security; and this is particularly so where it is thought that the house may be used in an unconventional way – i.e. part of it is sublet. The estate agent who steers West Indian house buyers into such housing types, therefore, also becomes important in guiding the purchaser to possible sources of finance. This means 'fringe operators' and mortgage brokers who charge high interest rates on relatively short term loans. The West Indian thus finds himself in what can only be described as a financial jungle, burdened with high repayments as well as rates, and probably substantial repair obligations. He can only survive by covering some of his costs from renting off part of his house. We thus arrive at a typical institution of West Indian housing in the inner parts of London – the owner-occupied multi-occupied houses, bringing together owner-occupiers and furnished tenants in the large older houses of the zones of transition.

R. Haddon *The Location of West Indians in the London Housing Market* 1970

1 What does R. Haddon mean when he calls the estate agent a 'gatekeeper'?

2 Why would the estate agents practise discrimination towards West Indian buyers? Why might it be in his or her interest to act as 'gatekeeper'?

3 In what ways are the houses in the 'twilight zone' different from those on the newer suburban estates further out of the city?

4 Why is the West Indian likely to be at a disadvantage even if there were no discrimination?

5 What effect has this pattern of housing purchase had on:
a the development of West Indian communities;
b integration of black Britons into the wider society?

33
Work

When a bird builds a nest or a spider a web, is it working? Is the human activity we call work the same as 'work' done by animals?

All forms of life sustain themselves on their natural environment; thus all conduct activities for the purpose of appropriating natural products to their own use. Plants absorb moisture, minerals and sunlight; animals feed on plant life or prey on other animals. But to seize upon the materials of nature ready made is not work; work is an activity that alters these materials from their natural state to improve their usefulness. The bird, the beaver, the spider, the bee, and the termite, in building nests, dams, webs, and hives, all may be said to work. Thus the human species shares with others the activity of acting upon nature in a manner which changes its forms to make them more suitable for its needs.

However, what is important about human work is not its similarities with that of other animals, but the crucial differences that mark it as the exact opposite. 'We are not now dealing with those primitive instinctive forms of labour that remind us of the mere animal,' wrote Marx in the first volume of *Capital*. 'We pre-suppose labour in a form that stamps it as exclusively human. A spider conducts operations that resemble those of a weaver, and a bee puts to shame many an architect in the construction of her cells. But what distinguishes the worst architect from the best of bees is this, that the architect raises his structure in imagination before he erects it in reality. At the end of every labour-process, we get a result that already existed in the imagination of the labourer at its commencement. He not only effects a change of form in the material on which he works, but he also realises a purpose of his own to which he must subordinate his will.'

Human work is conscious and purposive, while the work of other animals is instinctual. Instinctive activities are inborn rather than learned, and represent a relatively inflexible pattern for the release of energy upon the receipt of specific stimuli. It has been observed, for example, that a caterpillar which has completed half of its cocoon will continue to manufacture the second half without concern even if the first half is taken away. A more striking illustration of instinctual labour is seen in the following:

> The South African weaverbird builds a complicated nest of sticks, with a knotted strand of horsehair as foundation. A pair was isolated and bred for five generations under canaries, out of sight of their fellows and without their usual nest-building materials. In the sixth generation, still in captivity but with access to the right materials, they built a nest perfect even to the knot of horsehair.

Harry Braverman *Labour and Monopoly Capital* 1974

1 What do you understand by the following terms?
purposive
instinctual/instinctive
polar opposite
conscious
stimuli/stimulus

2 What evidence is given for the instinctual or 'inborn' character of work by birds and insects? What would you have expected the birds and insects to have done if their work was learned and purposive?

3 How does 'human work' differ from work in the 'animal world'?

4 Do you think that Braverman's view of human work completely adequate? Can you think of any examples of human activity which are 'purposive' but do not include 'work'?

5 How would you define work?

6 Is it possible to say which of the following activities are 'work'? Explain your answer.
a taking photographs
b cooking hamburgers
c playing football
d making furniture
e looking after children

7 Discuss in your class how you would distinguish between work and non-work activities.

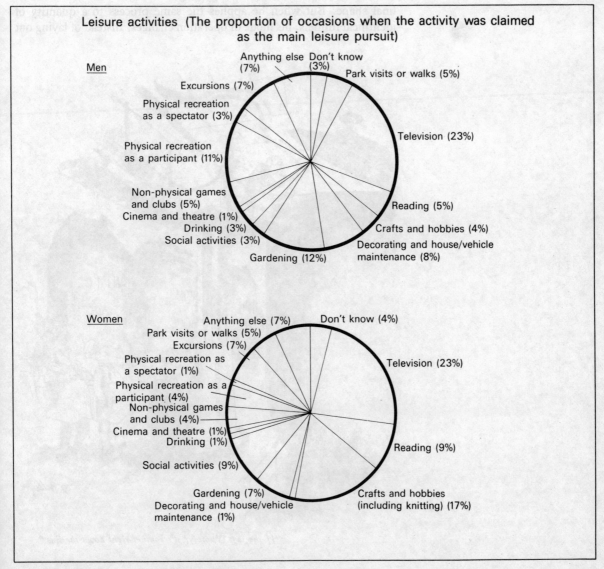

Leisure activities (The proportion of occasions when the activity was claimed as the main leisure pursuit)

Men

Anything else (7%)
Don't know (3%)
Park visits or walks (5%)
Excursions (7%)
Physical recreation as a spectator (3%)
Physical recreation as a participant (11%)
Television (23%)
Non-physical games and clubs (5%)
Cinema and theatre (1%)
Drinking (3%)
Social activities (3%)
Reading (5%)
Crafts and hobbies (4%)
Decorating and house/vehicle maintenance (8%)
Gardening (12%)

Women

Anything else (7%)
Don't know (4%)
Park visits or walks (5%)
Excursions (7%)
Physical recreation as a spectator (1%)
Physical recreation as a participant (4%)
Television (23%)
Non-physical games and clubs (4%)
Cinema and theatre (1%)
Drinking (1%)
Social activities (9%)
Reading (9%)
Gardening (7%)
Decorating and house/vehicle maintenance (1%)
Crafts and hobbies (including knitting) (17%)

Based on K.K. Sillitoe *Planning For Leisure* HMSO 1969

34
The division of labour

The division of labour is the basis for industrial production. Harry Braverman explains why:

The division of labour in production begins with the analysis of the labour process – that is to say, the separation of the work of production into its constituent elements. Such an analysis or separation, in fact, is characteristic of every labour process organised by workers to suit their own needs.

For example, a tinsmith makes a funnel: he draws the elevation view on sheetmetal, and from this develops the outline of an unrolled funnel and its bottom spout. He then cuts out each piece with snips and shears, rolls it to its proper shape, and crimps or rivets the seams. He then rolls the top edge, solders the seams, solders on a hanging ring, washes away the acid used in soldering, and rounds the funnel to its final shape. But when he applies the same process to a quantity of identical funnels, his mode of operation changes. Instead of laying out

"If she says 'Yummy,' it's bonuses right down the line."

the work directly on the material, he makes a pattern and uses it to mark off the total quantity of funnels needed; then he cuts them all out, one after the other, rolls them, etc. In this case, instead of making a single funnel in the course of an hour or two, he spends hours or even days on each step of the process, creating in each case fixtures, clamps, devices, etc. which would not be worth making for a single funnel but which, where a sufficiently large quantity of funnels is to be made, speed each step sufficiently so that the saving justifies the extra outlay of time. Quantities, he has discovered, will be produced with less trouble and greater economy of time in this way than by finishing each funnel individually before starting the next.

Such methods of analysis of the labour process and its division into constituent elements have always been and are to this day common in all trades and crafts and represent the first form of the subdivision of labour in detail. It is clear that they satisfy, essentially if not fully, the three advantages of the division of labour given by Adam Smith in his famous discussion in the first chapter of *The Wealth of Nations*:

> This great increase in the quantity of work, which, in consequence of the division of labour, the same number of people are capable of performing, is owing to three different circumstances; first, to the increase of dexterity in every particular workman; secondly, to the saving of the time which is commonly lost in passing from one species of work to another; and lastly, to the invention of a great number of machines which facilitate and abridge labour, and enable one man to do the work of many.

The example which Smith gives is the making of pins, and his description is as follows:

> One man draws out the wire, another straightening it, a third cuts it, a fourth points it, a fifth grinds it at the top for receiving the head; to make the head requires two or three distinct operations; to put it on, is a peculiar business, to whiten the pins is another; it is even a trade by itself to put them into the paper; and the important business of making a pin is, in this manner, divided into about eighteen distinct operations, which, in some manufactories, are all performed by distinct hands, though in others the same man will sometimes perform two or three of them.

In this example, the division of labour is carried one step further than in the example of the tinsmith. Not only are the operations separated from each other, but they are assigned to different workers. Here we have not just the analysis of the labour process but the creation of the detail worker. Both steps depend upon the scale of production: without sufficient quantities they are impracticable. Each step represents a saving in labour time. The greatest saving is found in the analysis of the process, and a further saving is to be found in the separation of operations among different workers.

The worker may break the process down, but he never voluntarily converts himself into a lifelong detail worker. This is the contribution of the capitalist, who sees no reason why, if so much is to be gained from the first step – analysis – and something more gained from the second – breakdown among workers – he should not take the second step as well as the first. That the first step breaks up only the process, while the second dismembers the worker as well, means nothing to the capitalist, and all the less since, in destroying the craft as a process under the control of the worker, he reconstitutes it as a process under his own control. He can now count his gains in a double sense, not only in productivity but in management control, since that which mortally injures the worker is in this case advantageous to him.

Harry Braverman *Labour and Monopoly Capital* 1974

"Doing me out of overtime's one thing—riding home with me Popsy's another."

1 What are the stages in making a funnel?

2 What differences would there be in making a large number of funnels?

3 Why would the tinsmith find it worthwhile making 'fixtures, clamps and devices' for making a number of funnels but not for just one funnel?

4 Adam Smith lists three advantages of the division of labour. What are they?

5 What is the main difference in the division of labour used by tinsmiths and the division of labour in Adam Smith's pin factory?

6 What are the two steps in the creation of 'the detail workers'?

7 What does Braverman mean when he writes 'Both steps depend upon the scale of production'?

8 In Braverman's view what function has the capitalist in the division of labour?

9 What are the advantages of the division of labour:
a to the capitalist;
b to the worker?
Are there any disadvantages?

35

The bakery

Many jobs are boring and repetitive. The work does not require any skill or concentration. Jason Ditton studied a group of workers in a bread factory:

Towards the end of a summer that I spent doing research in a factory bakery, a supervisor remarked: '. . . you take the blokes here . . . they clock-in and clock-out . . . no worries and no responsibility . . . Bob's your uncle isn't it? . . .' This new variation of a classic theme – how easy life is for the manual worker – ignores the difficult and not openly talked about problems of handling a working day, of lasting out from clocking-on to clocking-out, in the face of a soul-destroying and endless repetitiveness and monotony.

All of us sometimes find ourselves with pockets of time where we have to wait (for kettles to boil, for the telephone to ring) and we kill or fill this time with various inconsequential pastimes. But although everybody working in a bakery must somehow deal with such problems of time, the managerial career helps to structure life into a recognised pattern; and the upward movement between rungs on a promotion ladder turns time into a scarce resource rather than an empty residue. But the shopfloor workers do not share this 'linear' feeling of time. For them, work means a lifetime of waiting at machines where attendance is necessary, but full attention is not: a non-career situation with little control of personal time and physical movement. For the bakery workers, the continuous and unchanging production process, a literally neverending stream of bread pouring from the ovens, is broken up by the completion of periodic 'runs' of different sorts of bread. But the perpetual repetition of these runs year after year means that they become part of the sameness of work. Because work, for the operatives, cannot mark any significant career points, their perception of time and of the relationship between events, turns into a cyclical pattern within which movement occurs, but 'nothing' happens. When I last returned to the bakery for another bout of fieldwork, nothing, or so they told me, had happened in the three months that I had been away.

Faced with the difficulty of keeping research going under such monotonous work conditions, and of surviving endless days of mindless repetition, I began to envy the apparently unconcerned and uninterested way that the regulars worked. I only had to do three months: how could they survive, doing 'nothing' for a lifetime? It eventually became apparent that their carefree attitude concealed an unobservable and private world of the imagination: a 'through the looking glass' world of work.

The workers were individually placed between two complex sets of conveyor belts, transferring the dough at various stages of the baking process from one belt to another. Their arms and legs were necessarily a prisoner of the present, but their minds continually looked for, and found, escape. Work, for the men, was seen as the partial suspension of life, an endless part-time imprisonment. One worker, after misdating an important event in the social history of the bakery, sadly commented: 'You don't get no sense of time in this labour camp . . . not like in the outside world. . .' Filling the interminable present became an essential element in the battle to keep going to the end of the shift. One casual worker only managed to stick it out for ten hours before leaving: and another, who eventually got a job in a different department, recalled: '. . . that last hour . . . I didn't think I'd last out . . .'

The treadmill feeling of monotony, coupled with the cyclical sameness of repetitiveness, produces a complex and confused situation for the men. Sometimes, these problems seemed to be 'out there' ('it's so monotonous, that's why I feel tired') but on the other occasions they were explained as feelings 'in me' ('I dunno. . .I just don't seem to be able to get on with the job today'). Their own attempts to unravel these confusions unwittingly perpetuated the problems: few of the men believed their own experience was general, thinking their problems were unshared. Publicly, everybody agreed that the 'dough' was the easiest and best job: privately they schemed to work in the middle (where full tins are put into the oven), on the end of the oven, or on the revolving table, where the bread is racked up. One experienced worker said: 'I prefer the oven, too, funny isn't it, I dunno, the dough's easy. . .no, the oven's better somehow.' Another worker said: 'I dunno, it's not just how hard the work is, is it? It seems you've worked twice as long on there. It seems like there's some bugger standing on the hands of the clock and stopping them going round.'

Jason Ditton *Monotony at Work* 1972

1 What do you understand by the following terms?
managerial career
cyclical pattern
promotion ladder
monotonous work conditions

2 How was the division of labour arranged in the factory? What were the key stages in production?

3 In your own words describe what it was like to work in the bakery.

36

Housework

Work is often thought of as something that can only be done 'at work', in a factory or an office. For many women, however, 'work' is 'housework'. Ann Oakley has studied housework in the same way that other sociologists have studied 'factory work'. Here she compares three common features of the work experience – monotony, fragmentation, excessive pace.

A common charge levelled against housework is that it is monotonous and repetitive. Although the tasks that make up housework are dissimilar, there is said to be a 'sameness' about them which derives from their frequent need to be repeated, their lack of meaning, and the impermanence of what is achieved. There is nothing more 'automatic' than the perfect housewife, mechanically pursuing the same routine day in and day out. The Peckham Rye Women's Liberation Group speak from personal experience when they say that housework is:

An endless routine: it creates its own high moments of achievement and satisfaction so as to evade. . .futility. The bolt you tighten on the factory floor vanishes to be replaced by another: but the clean kitchen floor is tomorrow's dirty floor and the clean floor of the day after that. The appropriate symbol for housework (and for housework alone) is not the interminable conveyor belt but a compulsive circle like a pet mouse in its cage spinning round on its exercise wheel, unable to get off. . .

But the routine is never quite routine, so the vacuum in one's mind is never vacuous enough to be filled. 'Housework is a worm eating away at one's ideas. . .Like a fever dream it goes on and on, until you desperately hope that it can be all achieved in one blow. You lay the breakfast the night before, you have even been known to light the gas under the kettle for tomorrow's tea, wishing that by breakfast time everything could be over. . .'

The monotony of housework turns it into a mindless task. Without calling for one's whole attention, it so persistently demands a small part of it that concentration on anything else is ruled out. Thus monotony and fragmentation are intimately connected, and through the need to accomplish a long series of jobs each day, a feeling of always having too much to do may be added.

Is this a very one-sided picture, as it is sometimes claimed to be? Perhaps monotony, fragmentation and excessive pace are noted by few housewives and are not bound up with a dominant feeling of dissatisfaction. One way to test this possibility is to ask direct questions about these experiences in housework, and compare them with that reported by other groups of workers. In their study of attitudes to industrial work John Goldthorpe and his colleagues asked three questions designed specifically to measure the extent to which industrial work is experienced as unsatisfying. These questions were: 'Do you find your present job monotonous?' 'Do you find you can think about other things while doing your job?' and 'Do you ever find the pace of the job too fast?' On the basis of the answers they received to these questions

Goldthorpe and his colleagues concluded that monotony is a definite source of job dissatisfaction. Fragmentation and excessive pace were also found to be important variables bearing on job satisfaction. Many workers, who did not find their work monotonous, stated that it did not absorb their full attention or that they found the pace of it too fast. These three questions were used in an adapted form for housewives in the present sample.

When asked, 'Do you find housework monotonous on the whole?' 30 out of the 40 women said 'yes':

'It's the feeling that although you've done the job for today you've still go to do it tomorrow. It's one of the things that gets me down about it.' (Journalist's wife.)

Fragmentation – the experience of work subdivided into a series of unconnected tasks not requiring the worker's full attention – is also a common experience. Thirty-six of the forty women said 'yes' to the question 'Do you find you can think about other things while you're working?, and most of the women then went on to offer examples of topics they thought about. From these answers, it is clear that fragmentation is an expected and accepted quality of housework.

So far as the housewife is concerned, time limits imposed by factors outside her control mean that the pace of her work is too fast for each task to get the attention she would like to give it. Unlike many jobs, housework can often be done in a very short space of time without actually failing to be done at all. Cleaning may consist of a quick dust or 'whip round' for the harassed housewife, and to some eyes at least it will still look as though the house has been cleaned. However, it is the housewife's ultimate responsibility to see that all tasks get done properly.

To summarise therefore, monotony, fragmentation and time pressures are aspects of housework commonly experienced by housewives.

Table 4 The experience of monotony, fragmentation and speed in work: housewives and factory workers compared

Percentage experiencing:

Workers	Monotony	Fragmentation	Speed
Housewives	75	90	50
Factory workers*	41	70	31
Assembly line workers*	67	86	36

* These figures are taken from Goldthorpe et al *The Affluent Worker: Industrial Attitudes and Behaviour*, page 18. The assembly line workers are a sub-sample of the factory workers.

Ann Oakley *The Sociology of Housework* 1974

1 What is meant by fragmentation?

2 Unlike many workers the housewife does not have a boss or supervisor watching her to see that jobs are done on time, or a conveyor belt to set the pace of work. Why then did half of the housewives interviewed complain about the excessive pace of housework?

3 Which of the groups of workers studied experienced the greatest monotony, fragmentation and speed of work? Is this what you would have expected before reading the passage?

37

Status differences at work

In the late 1960s Dorothy Wedderburn conducted an enquiry into differences in the working conditions and terms of employment of male employees in 815 establishments. The table summarises her findings:

Table 5 Selected differences in terms and conditions of employment
in which the condition applies:

Percentage of establishments

	Manual employees	Non-manual employees			Management	
	Operatives	Foremen	Clerical workers	Technicians	Middle managers	Senior managers
Holidays: 15 days+	38	72	74	77	84	88
Choice of holiday time	35	54	76	76	84	88
Normal working 40+ hours per week	97	94	9	23	27	22
Sick pay – employers' scheme	57	94	98	97	98	98
Pension – employers' scheme	67	94	90	94	96	96
Time off with pay for personal reasons	29	84	83	86	91	93
Pay deductions for any lateness	90	20	8	11	1	0
Warning followed by dismissal for persistent lateness	84	66	78	71	48	41
No clocking-in or booking-in	2	46	48	45	81	94

Taking all employment conditions together from fringe benefits to discipline – our survey shows a big gulf between manual workers on the one hand and non-manual workers on the other. In every respect manual workers are worse off than their non-manual counterparts; and in many cases the differences are very large indeed. The data suggests that there may be another division with the non-manual employees such as foremen, draughtsmen and clerical workers as one group, and management as another. But even where these two non-manual groups diverge, they are still more like each other than they are like the manual workers.

The data suggest that the kind of treatment which the non-manual worker gets at work reflects an assumption by the employer that values are shared – that the non-manual worker will 'behave responsibly', will 'have the interests of the firm at heart' and 'not abuse privileges'. The manual worker is more often subject to formal rules and prescriptions. On the other hand, he is far more likely to work for an employer who recognises a trade union to negotiate on his behalf.

The wide inequalities revealed by this survey have important implications for the understanding of the employee's behaviour outside work. Differences in the length of the working week, in flexibility of timekeeping, in the constraints of shiftwork are important for the way a man can organise his social life. Manual workers may remain marked off by such difference.

Dorothy Wedderburn *Divisions in the Workplace* 1970

1 What do you understand by the following terms?
fringe benefits
diverge
converge
formal rules and prescriptions
negotiate
constraints

2 Use the table to find the following information. The percentage of establishments in which:
a technicians lose pay if they are late for work;
b middle managers have to sign-in when they arrive for work;

c operatives get paid by their employers if they are sick;
d a foreman is likely to be allowed time off with pay to attend a funeral;
e manual workers get a fortnight's holiday or less;
f clerical workers work more than 40 hours per week;
g middle managers lose pay if they arrive late for work;
h manual workers have to clock-in for work;
i retiring clerical workers receive a pension;
j foremen who regularly arrive late are likely to be sacked.

3 What assumptions do employers make about their 'non-manual' workers?

4 Do you think the same assumptions are made about manual workers? What evidence is there for your answer?

5 How can differences in conditions and terms of employment influence 'the employee's behaviour outside work'? Give examples.

38
Holidays

Going on holiday is the biggest 'leisure time' event in the year for many people. But the idea of an 'annual holiday' for all workers is fairly recent and is closely linked to the development of capitalist industry.

Barrie Newman sees the 'annual holiday' as a middle class invention which was only graduallly accepted as a necessity for all workers.

It was only in the mid-nineteenth century that work for the industrial workers began to be limited to regular hours, leaving a daily margin of time for leisure and gradually an increasing amount of holidays. As a regular feature of society, however, holidays may be said to have 'percolated' down to the lower strata. The earliest records of holidays in Britain reflect a concern with a return to nature and physical health, in particular with 'taking the waters'. Spa towns such as Bath and Tunbridge Wells were the main holiday resorts of the eighteenth century, their popularity remaining unchallenged until the emergence of seaside towns. A belief in the medical powers of salt water grew and this, together with the royal patronage of such towns as Brighton, established the vogue of holidaymaking by the sea. It was at such seaside towns that the taking of holidays was copied by, and became the accepted habit of, the middle class. It became the norm for middle class families and gradually those considered 'lower' middle class to spend a number of days away from home at the seaside.

As the middle class came to embrace the desirability of more and more travel, larger numbers of the lower middle class, who hitherto had spent very little time in this way, found themselves faced by small but not unimportant outlays on transport fares, not merely to and from their place of employment but elsewhere on leisure occasions, on excursions and, especially, for the purpose of their annual holiday. In this process, clear and dominant views emerged as to the acceptable standards and types of holidays. These views were based upon the imitation of the leisured class.

For the majority of workers, however, paid holidays remained uncommon. Holidays were thought to be for a minority, for those who had a formal education and a 'sense of responsibility', who were considered able to manage large amounts of leisure time. The belief persisted among this minority that leisure for the majority, where it existed, needed to be controlled and where granted, needed to be introduced in a very gradual way. Extensive leisure and holidays among the masses were often believed to encourage activities considered both dangerous and associated with degeneracy or, at best, to entail a frivolous dissipation of time.

It is not surprising then, that even in the 1930s less than two million workers had paid holidays. There were public holidays which, with the spread of railways, enabled many manual workers to go on a day's trip to the seaside, but it was not until 1938 and the Holidays with Pay Act that a framework was provided for a major extension in collective and voluntary agreements for paid holidays. The length of time it took to recognise the important link between the holiday and the health and morale of the work force is difficult to explain. Whatever the reason, however, it is clear that there was a change over from a 'burn-up policy' whereby workers were used up in the same way as machines and then scrapped, to the 'maintenance policy' where greater value was placed upon 'social capital' and where holidays were seen as a form of investment in workers. The evidence tends to show that the need for holidays arose partly from questions of health and efficiency and the abatement of industrial fatigue.

Barrie Newman *Holidays and Social Class* 1973

1 Where did the upper and middle classes take their holidays in the eighteenth century? What did they go there for?

2 For many years holidays were solely for a middle class minority. What beliefs about the nature of holidays served to keep it that way?

3 The development of cheap transport, improved wages and holidays with pay meant that the working classes could begin to take regular holidays. How was this linked to a changed attitude towards the workers?

4 'It can be argued that health has always been an underlying element in the development of holidays for all social classes.' What evidence is there to support this statement?

"Psst! . . . Real Ale?"

McLACHLAN

39
Retirement

The change from an active worker to a retired pensioner is one of the most significant changes of status in our lives. It often involves a considerable loss of income as well as changes in status and lifestyle. Jeremy Tunstall describes the lives of retired fishermen in Hull in the early 1960s.

Fishermen, because of their long periods of absence at sea, have less close ties with ordinary people than do most men and thus retirement for them produces a correspondingly greater tragedy. Moreover fishermen when at work are one of the poorest groups in our country – if the total sufferings and rewards of their life are taken into account. Consequently retired or 'beached' fishermen, as they forlornly call themselves, can be described as one of the poorest of all groups living among us, in economic as well as social terms.

When they are at sea fishermen bewail the fact that no pension awaits them and that they will probably end their lives as watchmen on trawlers in the dock, earning a mere pittance. Some men leave the job around the age of forty and get themselves a low-paying but secure job on the shore. But most men, fearful of going back to a labourer's job ashore, continue to go to sea as long as they can manage to get a berth on a trawler.

Out of the 55 men, 5 were living on the old age pension, 8 were unemployed and 41 were working. The pensioners had not stopped working willingly, and filled in the question asking how long they had been out of work, indicating that they considered themselves as being unemployed and the pension as just another kind of dole. One of them said: 'It's a crime to grow old on the fish-dock' and this summed up the others' attitude.

Three men worked as seamen on lightships. The hours in this job are long, but the wages are about average for ex-fishermen and the job has a comparatively high degree of security. A lightshipman feels himself to be quite lucky, in spite of being paid only 2s 6d. (12½p) per hour.

Even if he has a job the ex-fisherman now has too little money to go out very often, and if unemployed he must spend long hours at home. Repeatedly men stress the simple benefits of home life:

'All the things that one has missed after doing 35 years at sea, such as the home comforts, value of family life.'
'I am more contented, as you have more home life and every night in bed makes the life worth living.'
'After 40 years at sea like a fish out of water, a different life altogether, but gradually adjusting oneself to it. Had family of seven, but stopped going to sea when last daughter got married. (My average money cut by half, now as relief engineer on dock £11 per week, £9 17s (£9.85) to take home.) Wife and I just getting to know one another.'
'I think the rough life on trawlers (I mean in those days) makes a man value home life and the love and comfort there is in the world.'

This changed attitude to home comes about not because the ex-fisherman's capacity to love his life and home suddenly changes spontaneously, but because the circumstances of his life change, his horizons shrink. However, the wife's life, which is usually based on housework, cooking, perhaps part-time work, and social contact with the daughter and other relatives, does not change suddenly and cannot be expected to blossom forth into quite the same new-found appreciation of her fisherman husband.

Some old fishermen hang around the Hessle Road pubs and clubs, and when you go in for a drink with a group of young fishermen it's surprising how frequently you meet their fathers, uncles, fathers-in-law, or other relatives – presumably because these men intentionally go in there when they know the young men have landed. The youths gallantly buy the old men drinks, pass a backhander under the table and perhaps slap down a coin with the barman for one more drink for the old man as they move off to the waiting taxi. But other old men sit by themselves quietly eking out a pint of mild for as long as possible.

Some attend subsidised social meetings on Hessle Road to while away the hours. One such meeting was the work of a churchgoing woman who owned a prosperous local shop. She provided the old men with a place to meet, tables and chairs for playing games, and tea at a penny a cup. The men came every afternoon of the week in contrast to the old women who only came twice. The women chatted endlessly about their families, their grandchildren and great-grandchildren and domestic problems such as the difficulty of living in an inconveniently large house now that the children had left. The men were much more formal, playing dominoes right through the afternoon – and sadly restrained compared with young fishermen crowded into a trawler's mess deck eagerly gambling their settlings as they steamed back from Iceland.

Those who are humble enough to accept the charity of others do so in pubs and clubs. Some wait alone for death at home, proud and defiant, while others stay indoors and thankfully accept the help of their children. One old fisherman living alone in a terrace house said:

'The bairns gave me this TV set. Without it I'd have been dead by now. Things are much better than they used to be.'

This is the way the fishermen's world ends.

Jeremy Tunstall *The Fishermen* 1962

1 Make a list of the ways retirement changed the fisherman's way of life.

2 Sociologists have described retirement as a 'status passage' – a time when the individual moves from one status to another. How does the fisherman's status change on retirement? How does the change in status affect his view of life?

3 Fishing is an extreme occupation which is very different from most other jobs. How far do you think retiring from a life as a fisherman in 1960 is likely to be different from retirement in any other career today? In your answer you should consider the following aspects:
a pension
b home life
c social activities
d relationships with kin.

40

The borough council

Two studies of the Oxfordshire town of Banbury were carried out between 1948 and 1951 and between 1966 and 1969. The working of the local Borough Council was one of the areas studied as this extract from the second study shows:

The Borough Council is composed of elected representatives of opposed political parties. Nevertheless, in many ways the councillors are a united group. They have a common task to perform in running the town. It was interesting in the middle 'forties to observe the gradual change of attitude of the newly elected Labour councillors towards their opponents, whom they not only met face to face for the first time but in a situation in which they shared executive responsibility. Over time councillors came to share experiences and traditions; both sides accept the legitimacy of the council procedures. The jokes they share are often unintelligible to outsiders.

In the Council Chamber, when councillors know they are being observed and recorded – when they are 'on-stage', they occasionally give expression to party political differences. Nevertheless there remains an observable air of unanimity. When they are 'back-stage' this unity is even more observable.

At election counts, for example, all councillors are usually present and each candidate can appoint up to three scrutineers. The public and press are excluded. There is friendly and informal interaction between members of the opposing parties. Little groups earnestly discuss committee business, the dismissal of a car park attendant, for example. There is also a good deal of joking, each side assuring the other that they have won marginal wards by impossible majorities. Opponents join in a common condemnation of the electorate for its apathy. As the results gradually become known, the joking begins to develop an unkind edge.

The results are first declared inside the town hall to the candidates and their scrutineers. They all go downstairs for the formal declaration to the public and the press. The assembled public are supporters of the candidates. The politicians no longer speak to each other. Indeed they become partisan and expression is given to extreme differences of opinion. There is booing and cheering and occasional bursts of the 'Red Flag'. The change is notable. Councillors are public opponents but collaborators in running the town. In this they are friendly and cooperative, but the joking relationships cover, and also reveal, their awareness of their political differences. For most of the time, the two political parties work together quite cordially: divisions on matters of principle are rare. Usually voting is on party lines without the formal application of the 'whip'. Sometimes Labour and Conservative councillors vote with the opposite party. There has only been one expulsion from either political group since 1950.

The atmosphere of friendship and day-to-day comradeship conceals marked differences of emphasis. The Conservatives as 'guardians of the rates' tend to oppose increased public spending, while the Labour councillors are generally in favour of 'laying out money in the public

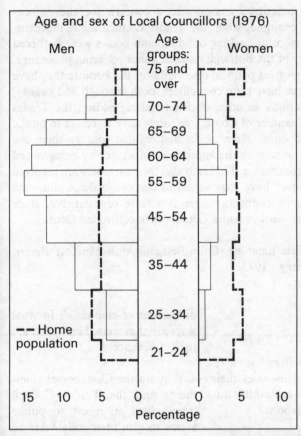

Age and sex of Local Councillors (1976)

Men   Age groups: Women
             75 and over
             70–74
             65–69
             60–64
             55–59
             45–54
             35–44
             25–34
             21–24

- - Home population

15 10 5 0   0 5 10
Percentage

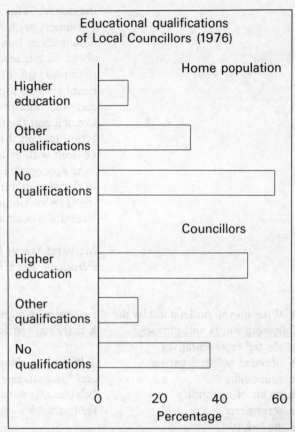

Educational qualifications of Local Councillors (1976)

Home population

Higher education

Other qualifications

No qualifications

Councillors

Higher education

Other qualifications

No qualifications

0   20   40   60
Percentage

Source: *Social Trends*

interest'. These differences are kept alive by the party ideologies and the different backgrounds of the councillors. Furthermore, councillors from opposing parties do not share each other's company in whatever spare time Council business may have left them.

The councillors act in concert in relation to outside bodies. Thus, when they initiated a public meeting in 1966, just after the fieldwork started, to discuss the proposal to expand the town to 70,000, councillors agreed that they would not take part in the discussion. They agreed to accept the Chairman of the Development Committee as their spokesman. In the event, one of the councillors broke the agreement and spoke strongly against expansion and in favour of a referendum on the issue. The Council spokesman had already rejected this notion. In this case, it would seem that the councillor's loyalty to groups other than the Council overcame her loyalty to her fellow councillors, and also to a leader of her party. It is rare for councillors to show in public that other loyalties are more important than loyalty to the Council.

The old-established pressure groups in the town undoubtedly influence the councillors. The Chamber of Commerce and the Trades Council in a sense represent the interests of industry and commerce: the former from the side of proprietors and managers, and the latter from the side of the employees. Both bodies operate on a broad front and do not concern themselves exclusively with the interests of their members narrowly conceived, having in addition a concern for the 'good of the town'. This sometimes amounts to a concern for the citizen-consumer, as, for example, when the Trades Council made representations about bus stops or parking or when both bodies were bothered about the efficiency of the Borough Council's snow-clearing procedure. Both make quite frequent political interventions, but because they have members who are or have been councillors (both borough and county) and who hold positions on other decision-making bodies, the Trades Council and the Chamber of Commerce rarely have to resort to public action to gain their ends. Many of the matters that concern them can be dealt with by a word with the appropriate official or by being raised in an appropriate committee. That is to say, their members are involved in decision-making or have easy access to decision-makers, although the Trades Council's connections are less close or extensive, since Banbury has almost always had a Conservative-controlled Council.

Margaret Stacy, Eric Batstone, Colin Bell and Anne Murcott *Power, Persistence and Change* 1975

1 What do you understand by the following words and phrases?
a elected representatives
b opposed political parties
c councillors
d an air of unanimity
e scrutineers
f the 'whip'
g party ideologies
h act in concert
i referendum
j pressure groups
k marginal wards

2 When are councillors 'on-stage' and 'back-stage'? How does their behaviour towards each other differ in the two situations?

3 How would you explain the viewpoint that the borough councillors are 'a united group with differences of emphasis'. In what ways are they united and what are their differences?

4 Why do the Chamber of Commerce and the Trades Council 'rarely have to resort to public action to gain their ends'? Are all pressure groups in the same position?

41
Voters and parties

Over long periods of time the pattern of voting in any country changes. In twentieth century Britain the Liberal party has declined and the Labour Party has emerged. In the shorter period of time other changes occur with new parties appearing and elections swinging from one party to another. Finding out why people vote for particular parties and, more importantly, why they change their votes, is a problem for the political sociologist. Anthony King and Peter Kellner consider the evidence that has been presented on this issue.

Most voters have acquired some sort of party affiliation by the time they are about 30 or 35; the young are much more changeable politically than the middle aged and old. But where do the young acquire their partisan loyalties from? The obvious answer is 'from their parents'. And the obvious answer is partly true, but only partly. As Butler and Stokes put it, 'Partisanship over the individual's lifetime has some of the quality of a photographic reproduction that deteriorates with time: it is a fairly sharp copy of the parents' original at the beginning of political awareness, but over the years it becomes somewhat blurred, although remaining easily recognisable.'

What causes the blurring? If the family is thought of as one contender for the child's political allegiance, it would seem that it can have two main rivals. One is social class, where the party the parents support is not the party dominant in their class (i.e. where the parents are middle class socialists or working class Tories). The other is the political circumstances of the era in which the child grew up, where these run counter to the allegiance of the parents.

Butler and Stokes found that, whereas 85 per cent of children whose parents supported the dominant party in their class supported the same party themselves, only 58 per cent of the children whose parents supported the opposite party remained true to their parents' political faith; the other 42 per cent had been drawn away. Children were also likely to differ from their parents if, for example, their parents were Conservative at a time of great Labour strength like the years after 1945.

This raises, of course, the relationship between partisanship and age. The young at the moment (1972) are disproportionately Labour, the old disproportionately Conservative, with the middle aged tending to fall somewhere in between. The findings in the table below, which are typical of the last decade, are drawn from NOP's 1970 post-election survey:

Table 6   Voting by age, 1970

	18–24	25–34	35–44	45–54	55–64	65+
Conservative	42.3	41.0	46.1	43.3	47.5	56.2
Labour	47.2	45.8	40.6	49.1	43.7	37.1

But, as Philip Abrams points out in *Age and generation*, although these facts are clear, the explanation for them is less so. The popularly held view is that people, as they grow older, become more Conservative – with a capital 'C'. And this view is rather compelling: the old are apt to be set in their ways, and everyone can think of a friend or uncle who was radical in his youth (or claims he was), but who now votes Tory. But a much better explanation is one in terms of 'political generations'.

On this view, the preponderance of Conservatives among the over-65s is the result, not primarily of their being old as such, but of their having matured politically at a time when the Conservatives were the dominant party, and when Labour was only beginning to emerge as a political force. The old, in other words, may always be conservative, in the sense of being set in their ways politically; but they will not indefinitely be Conservative. The greater political constancy of old people emerges clearly from Table 7, taken from Butler/Stokes. The dates in the top row are the dates at which respondents were first able to vote:

Table 7 Voting constancy and age

	pre-1981	inter-war	post-1945	post-1951
% supporting same party in 1959 and 1964	86	81	79	58

The photographic reproduction, showing how far children's voting resembles their parents, will naturally be especially blurred if the original photo itself was not very clear. Children are particularly prone to differ from their parents politically if they do not know which party their parents supported, or if their parents were divided. Under these circumstances children are usually drawn towards the party of their class.

Anthony King   *A Sociological Portrait: Politics*   1972

Charting Labour's decline is one thing: explaining it another. A team from the London School of Economics, led by Professor Hilde Himmelweit, have conducted probably the longest study of how a single group of voters' attitudes evolve. They contacted a range of school-children in 1951 and re-interviewed them until 1974.

The LSE team believe their evidence demolishes the notion that political behaviour is any longer chiefly determined by social class: rather, voters now choose which party they vote for rather in the manner of consumers going shopping. The trouble with Labour, on this analysis, is that it has depended too much and for too long on brand loyalty (i.e. working class electors voting for the working class party), at a time when the impact of wider education, greater social mobility and the translation of politics from being a community-based activity to a media-based activity have all encouraged voters to 'shop around'.

And, or course, when shopping around becomes a widespread habit, the prospects for a new 'brand', or political party, improve.

The LSE team found that they could predict an elector's vote at a general election far more accurately from knowing his or her attitudes to specific issues, than from knowing his or her class. And working class voters' attitudes to issues have grown out of line with Labour's.

The LSE team explain this largely in terms of social changes – voters are different people, acting in a different kind of world from 20 or 30 years ago. But, as John Goldthorpe, principal author of the massive Nuffield study of social mobility, argues, you cannot explain everything this way: if you are to construct a consumer model of voter behaviour you must also look at the products – the parties.

Labour's main failing, Goldthorpe reckons, is that 'it has failed to construct a new form of class politics'. In Sweden or France, where similar social developments to Britain have occurred, left-wing parties have found new issues on which they can campaign to win working class support – where white collar and blue collar workers can make common cause, such as with worker participation in management, and policies to ensure that banks and pension funds channel money into industry.

Peter Kellner *New Statesman* 1981

1 Which of the following statements are true or false?
a As you grow old you become more conservative
b Children always vote for the party of their parents
c Social class has no real influence over voting behaviour
d Social changes in things like education, social mobility and the media are likely to influence voting patterns

e Voting patterns depend on 'brand loyalty' for a particular party.

2 Write a paragraph on each of the following to explain how it might affect the way an individual votes:
a Family
b Social class
c Political generation
d 'Shopping around'

3 What views have each of the following contributed to the debate on this issue?
a Donald Butler and Donald Stokes
b Philip Abrams
c Hilde Himmelweit
d John Goldthorpe.

42

A fall at the committee fence

The story begins in 1971. The Totalisator Board, which runs the Tote on behalf of the government, had been doing so badly for two years it had been unable to pay its levy. The Tote was restricted to operating on racecourses, and with a combination of declining attendances, higher expenses, and feeble management, found it could only just cover its overheads.

In 1970 a former customs and excise commissioner, Mr Arthur Taylor, was made head of the Tote with a brief to correct the situation. He soon wrote to the Home Office saying that the Tote could only get back on its feet if it was allowed to enter the increasingly lucrative field of off-course betting, which at that time had a turnover of about £900 million a year, and was controlled by private bookmakers.

Home Office officials were rapidly convinced of the Tote's case, as was Lord Wigg, at that time chairman of the Horserace Betting Levy Board. So was Mr Reginald Maudling who was Home Secretary. Maudling was persuaded of the urgency of the Bill, and the Cabinet agreed. The Bill was introduced into the House on 12 November 1971, and came as a complete surprise, both to the Tory backbenchers, and to the bookmakers themselves. They were horrified at the implication for them and equally shocked by the fact that they had had no advance warning whatever.

The National Association of Bookmakers (NAB) moved fast. Almost immediately they set up a parliamentary action committee. Within days invitations had gone out to every MP to hear the bookies' case at a series of slap-up lunches. Tories were taken to the Mirabelle on December 2 and 8, and Labour MPs to the Park Lane on December 7 and 9. Immediately the Bill hit its first major controversy: Labour MPs vigorously complained that the Park Lane was not as expensive as the Mirabelle.

The lunches aroused a good deal of comment at the time. The *Daily Mail* called them 'one of the most blatant acts of lobbying', and the late Sir Gerald Nabarro tore his invitation up, calling it 'naked bribery'. In fact, many MPs were utterly unimpressed by the bookies' heavy-handedness. 'That just isn't the way things work round here,' one MP told us.

Nevertheless, the bookies must have been well pleased. On December 9, the day after the second lunch for Tories, it was reported that Mr Maudling faced a serious backbench revolt, and was preparing to tone the Bill down. Four days later, he faced an angry meeting of the Tory backbench 1922 committee, attended by about 50 MPs, and told them 'the Bill is no joy to me'. He hinted strongly at changes, saying that he would consider any alternative proposals submitted to him.

Meanwhile, the bookies decided to keep the pressure up. The NAB wrote to all its members asking them in turn to write to their MPs complaining about the Bill, and at the same time appealed for money to keep the national campaign going. At the end of January, they held another series of lunches for MPs, then on February 1 and 2, held two lavish drinks receptions in the House of Commons. The Bill was to get its second reading in the House the following day – February 3.

It would be nonsense to suggest that MPs were in any way 'bribed' by all this entertainment. Most tend to scoff at such obvious tactics. But the parties and lunches did give the bookies a golden chance to expound their case, which less prosperous lobbyists must do without.

The keenest supporters of the Bill, though they were disturbed by the sheer weight of the bookies' lobbying, remained absolutely confident that it would get through. It is indeed very rare for a Bill introduced by the Government with opposition backing to fail in its purpose.

In the debate perhaps the most effective speech came from the Labour member for Birmingham All Saints, Mr Brian Walden. Mr Walden's arguments presented a powerful rebuttal of the purpose of the Bill when it came to discussion in committee in April, but the first decisive attack on it came from an unexpected quarter, the chairman of the Horserace Betting Levy Board, Lord Wigg. He raised doubts at a meeting of the Levy Board and he spelled out to Mr Mark Carlisle of the Home Office why he could no longer support the Bill as it stood. At the end of the month *Sporting Life* led off with a frontal attack by Lord Wigg complaining that the Bill would skin the bookies alive.

Meanwhile, Mr Walden was presenting a powerful case against the Bill in the committee. The committee began meeting in April, and all its sittings were attended by representatives of the bookmakers. In May, a group of them approached Mr Walden and suggested that he worked on their behalf. Mr Walden replied that he would consider this, providing he got his own terms, including a five year contract as a consultant, and he would not be asked to lobby MPs or to organise functions.

On May 11 he told the committee that it was likely that he would have a financial interest with the NAB. Through the committee stage, the Government, through Mr Mark Carlisle, made a number of minor alterations to the Bill. But these were small technicalities and the spirit of the Bill remained intact. The document which the committee sent back to the House was substantially the same as the original Bill.

This was then the crucial time for the Bill. The Government was still unhappy with it, largely because of the mounting evidence that the Tote's difficulties were not as great as had been thought. Supporters of the Bill, however, felt it had to go through in order to give the public a real stake in off-course betting.

Mr Carlisle was looking round for ways in which to support the Tote without giving it this toehold in the bookies' field. In July, in the course of a number of chats, Mr Walden brought word from the bookies to Mr Carlisle. If the government did not implement certain clauses of the Bill, he said, the bookies would be prepared to give the Tote facilities in their shops for a Tote bet.

After Mr Carlisle had received assurance from the bookies that they would not attempt to prevent the Tote from buying existing bookies' licenses, the Government changed clause 3 by putting in an extra paragraph:

'This section shall not come into force unless and until the Secretary of State so directs by order made by statutory instrument.'

This meant that the Tote could not set up in direct competition on favourable terms, and the Bill was, in effect, dead.

The third reading was held on August 7. A number of bookies had places in the 'jury box', a row of benches on the floor of the House, just behind the Bar. When one of the chief supporters of the original bill, Mr Joe Ashton, came in, the bookies told him, 'You've lost.' In disgust, Mr Ashton left without making the speech he had planned to deliver, and the Bill was passed without a division.

The Guardian 1974

1 Write a summary of the methods used by the private bookmakers' lobby to stop the Bill on offcourse betting becoming law.

2 Compare this example of a pressure group with the community group described in 'People power' on page 114.

"My Harry got so confused he posted his ballot paper to Littlewoods and stuck his eight draws in your box!"

43
'Yes Minister'

For most people their only contact with a government minister is when they see one on television or read the newspaper. What are ministers and what do they do? Des Wilson describes the minister's job.

Let us look at the different roles a minister has to play:

First, as head of his department, he is responsible for the overall policy decisions – for giving his department a sense of direction. This calls for a clear grasp of the subject, for he often has to balance the conflicting views of civil servants, of members of his political party, and of all sorts of pressure groups outside Westminster and Whitehall. The minister is totally responsible to the Prime Minister and to the House of Commons for the activities of his department, and if its policies fail, or its decisions are proved to be unpopular, the minister must carry the can. He is the public face of his department – the man who defends it against public criticism, answers questions in the House of Commons, tables legislation and leads the fight to get parliament to pass it. At Cabinet meetings he has to represent the interests of his department, particularly when it comes to the sharing out of public money. All of this is intensely political.

Second, as a member of the Cabinet, a senior minister has to share in the responsibility for the overall government of the country, being sufficiently well briefed on all national problems, and the policies being pursued to solve them, to make an intelligent contribution to Cabinet discussions, to share in major decisions and to defend the government effectively wherever he or she is called upon to do so.

Third, the minister has the same responsibility as every other member of parliament – to be there to vote at key times, and to undertake all the responsibilities that MPs have to their constituents.

Fourth, he has his responsibilities to the party itself, to take part in its political affairs, attend its annual conference, and keep in close touch with his own local constituency party. He has to report to the parliamentary party and pay attention to what his colleagues in the House of Commons have to say about his ministerial job.

The balancing of all of these responsibilities, with the problems of keeping the confidence of the Prime Minister, the Cabinet, his civil servants, the House of Commons and his constituents, requires a wide range of qualities. A good minister must be a leader of men, an expert in public relations, a skilful parliamentary debater, and have a mind able to grasp the complicated detail of his departmental brief and at the same time define priorities and take an overall view. He has to have stamina, for the workload is tremendous and the pressure unceasing. He has to have good judgement, clarity of thought and vision, courage, the ability to conciliate, and personal authority. Not surprisingly, such men and women are scarce. Often a minister has been brilliant at grasping departmental detail and yet a disaster in the job, because of his inability to handle questioning and debate in the House of Commons or in public. Sometimes the reverse had been the position – a minister has been poor in his management of the department, but extremely good at political and public relations. Sometimes a minister seems strong to the outside world, but is weak within his department, falling within the power of the civil servants and ending up as little more than a front man for powerful men and women in Whitehall, who are not directly publicly accountable.

Des Wilson *So you want to be a Prime Minister 1979*

1 What is the meaning of the following terms?
civil servants
pressure group
legislation
cabinet
constituency
departmental brief

2 What are the four roles played by a senior minister? Which of these roles are shared with other members of parliament?

3 In what ways is the minister responsible for his department?

4 What are the qualities Des Wilson feels a good minister should have?

5 Who are the ministers, sometimes called Secretaries of State, who are in charge of the following government departments?
Department of Education and Science
Department of Health and Social Security
Foreign Office
Home Office
Department of Industry
Department of the Environment

"I don't know how you got into this country, old boy, but in this house everybody votes Conservative!"

44
The civil service

More than a decade ago the Fulton Committee reported on the super-ficiality of the gifted amateur who entered the civil service. Fulton wanted to create an administration that was less elitist, less amateurish and more professional. If the statistics are anything to go by the Fulton recommendations went largely unheeded. The Civil Service Commission still recruits in its own image and still shows a heavy preference for certain literary and oral skills helped in part by the method of selection and the high marks awarded at the final selection board. Comparing the period 1966–8 with the period 1975–7 the number of Oxbridge graduates as a percentage of external recruits to the administrative grade rose slightly (62 per cent to 63 per cent); whilst the proportion of arts graduates fell (59 per cent to 56 per cent). The number of specialists moving into the ranks of under secretary and above remained about constant at about 40 per cent throughout the period.

The establishment is unabashed by these statistics. First they argue that all that they show is a statistical bias. Then when challenged about that curious response, since any measurable bias is a statistical bias, they go on to say that figures merely indicate an educational bias, i.e. the people with the best brains who are most fitted to govern the country go to public schools and Oxford and Cambridge and there is nothing they can or should do about that. In short it is the belief of the establishment that the best people, as conventionally defined through certain types of degrees, are those best suited to govern the country. I do not believe it. If they are the best people and can adapt to anything, why must they be civil servants? Why should they not become plant managers in manufacturing industry upon whose ability Britain's future depends? And if it is true that they are the best people to govern the country, why is it that we are so badly governed by every test – economic management, economic success, social cohesion, social reform, international influence and so on?

Brian Sedgemore *The Secret Constitution* 1980

Table 8   Administration trainees – social background
1975

| Social class | Male | | Female | | |
	Applicants	Appointees	Applicants	Appointees	Population as a whole
	%	%	%	%	
I	19.6	25.9	21.9	23.1	
II	43.2	50.3	48.7	59.6	
Totals I & II	62.8	76.2	70.6	82.7	39*
III & V	37.2	23.8	29.4	17.3	61*

* Estimate

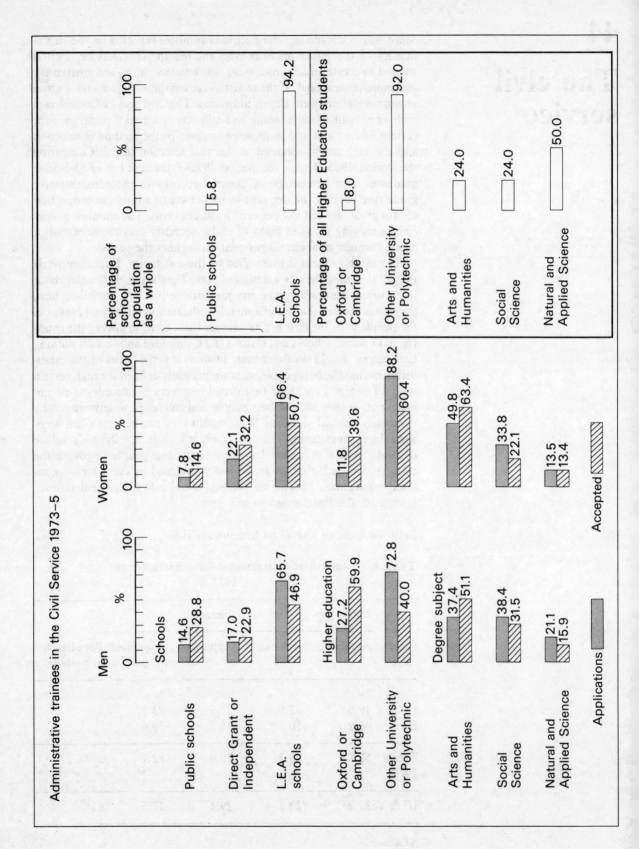

Administrative trainees in the Civil Service 1973–5

Men

Schools

	%	
Public schools	14.6	28.8
Direct Grant or Independent	17.0	22.9
L.E.A. schools	65.7	46.9

Higher education

Oxford or Cambridge	27.2	59.9
Other University or Polytechnic	72.8	40.0

Degree subject

Arts and Humanities	37.4	51.1
Social Science	38.4	31.5
Natural and Applied Science	21.1	15.9

Women

Schools

	%	
Public schools	7.8	14.6
Direct Grant or Independent	22.1	32.2
L.E.A. schools	66.4	50.7

Higher education

Oxford or Cambridge	11.8	39.6
Other University or Polytechnic	88.2	60.4

Degree subject

Arts and Humanities	49.8	63.4
Social Science	33.8	22.1
Natural and Applied Science	13.5	13.4

Applications   Accepted

Percentage of school population as a whole

	%
Public schools	5.8
L.E.A. schools	94.2

Percentage of all Higher Education students

Oxford or Cambridge	8.0
Other University or Polytechnic	92.0
Arts and Humanities	24.0
Social Science	24.0
Natural and Applied Science	50.0

Table 9 Graduate applicants for executive officer or equivalent 1973–5

	Male Applicants %	Appointees %	Female Applicants %	Appointees %
School:				
Public school/ direct grant etc.	18.0	19.3	15.9	14.9
LEA	75.8	74.7	79.6	81.6
University:				
Oxford/Cambridge	5.7	6.6	1.2	1.2
Other university/ polytechnic	94.3	93.4	98.8	98.8
Degree:				
Arts	27.0	29.8	46.1	48.7
Social sciences	36.4	36.1	33.6	33.8
Natural and applied sciences	34.8	32.5	17.9	15.7

Note: some categories are excluded and totals do not necessarily total 100.

Adapted from Brian Sedgemore *The Secret Constitution* 1980

1 Why does Brian Sedgemore believe that the Fulton recommendations went largely unheeded?

2 How does the civil service establishment explain the 'statistical bias' of the evidence on the recruitment of Oxbridge (Oxford and Cambridge) graduates?

3 Using the evidence in the graphs and tables to help you, sort out the following applicants into those that were more likely or less likely to become administrative trainees in the civil service in the period 1973–5.

a A young man who has been to public school.

b A young woman with a degree from Cambridge.

c Someone with a degree in sociology.

d The daughter of a manual worker.

e A young woman who went to an LEA school.

f Someone with an arts or humanities degree.

g A young woman or man with a degree from a polytechnic.

4 Compare the graphs on administrative trainees with the table on the lower status group of executive officers. What differences are there?

5 In your own words describe the backgrounds of:
a a typical administrative trainee;
b a typical executive officer.

45
Voting and youth

Are young people likely to have a different view of politics from their elders? Is the 'youth vote' something that political parties need to consider? How should schools encourage political awareness?

I was one of the 18 to 21 year olds who first had the vote in a general election in 1970. A Speaker's conference on electoral law had previously proposed a reduction in the minimum voting age to 20. Folk wisdom had it that wily old Harold Wilson had enfranchised the young like us in the confident expectation that the class of '68 would deliver for Labour in the polls.

The gratitude of young voters was expected to tip delicate balances in Labour's favour. When a court ruling gave students – one section of the new electorate – the right to register as voters in their town of study, it was the Conservatives who protested, and Labour who rubbed their hands in glee.

The early signs seemed to bear the parties out. In the spring local elections of 1970, for instance, Conservative territories in university towns – like north Oxford ward, where I myself lived – went Labour for the first time ever. Elsewhere, safe Tory wards suddenly became marginal. It seemed clear at least that the student vote had turned out for Labour.

Such research as does exist suggests that young people are still rather more likely than the electorate as a whole to support the Labour Party. In the summer of 1978, National Opinion Polls conducted a survey for the Jimmy Young programme among 15 to 21 year olds. At a time when the general tide in the polls indicated a 5 per cent Conservative lead, this showed a 2 per cent lead for Labour. NOP's figures for young voters – with the general results in brackets – were: Labour 44 per cent (42), Conservative 42 (47), Liberal 7 (8), Nationalists 5 (2), National Front 1 (0), others 1 (1). One month before the Tory landslide of 1979 the *News of the World* published a Marplan poll of 18 to 22 year olds. It showed a 2 per cent Conservative lead over Labour, with a 51–41 per cent split among women, helping the Tories overcome a 44–48 per cent deficit among men. At a time when the national polls showed Conservative leads of between 8 and 21 per cent this was still a strong Labour showing. Why should this be?

NOP found that 'political awareness among the young is fairly low'. Only 30 per cent of their sample claimed to be interested in politics, much lower than the normal adult proportion. However – not surprisingly – they found greater political interest among 18–21s than among 15–17s. Their conclusions tend to confirm the results of a poll of 15–16 year olds conducted in 1975 on behalf of the Hansard Society. On the basis of research with 4,027 schoolchildren it concluded that over four-fifths of the sample 'are insufficiently well-informed about local, national and international politics to know not only what is happening, but also how they are affected by it, and what they can do about it.'

All of the political parties believe in the existence of the 'youth vote'. They go after the women's vote, the union vote, the black vote and may establish special organisations to win these. In the same way they devote considerable resources to youth. For the youth vote is very large. Just over 32 per cent of voters are under 35 years old; 13 per cent are younger than 25. Each year a little over 550,000 new young voters come onto the electoral register.

Is it simply that young voters' preferences for Labour still reflect the credit the party acquired in the late sixties by giving the vote to 18 year olds, and by presiding over an era of genuine youth emancipation in several fields?

An examination of the detailed evidence of the polls suggests that Labour has no real claim to young voters' allegiance. Its strength may be more an indication of Tory weaknesses and misjudgements, which are not bound to continue indefinitely.

But if the youth vote is leaving the Labour stable, it will be fascinating to see whether it heads immediately for the Conservatives or to the open pastures of political apathy.

Martin Kettle *New Society* 1979

1 How do the political attitudes of young people differ from those of older people?

2 Is the 'youth vote' likely to be important to the political parties? What do the parties do to encourage young people to join them?

3 Does the evidence on youth voting support the views of the influence of age on voting on page 99.

4 What can schools do to make young people more aware of political issues? Should schools include politics in the curriculum for all pupils?

46

Who needs opinion polls?

Opinion polls are often used to find out what people think about political issues or the popularity of particular political parties. How accurate are these polls? Do they really tell us what people think?

What do opinion polls prove? The answer is that they prove nothing one way or the other. The testimony of opinion polls is unreliable – and not just the testimony of this or that opinion poll, mind, but *any* opinion poll. All opinion polls are bad.

Morally speaking, opinion polls are always an embarrassment. Touted as representing public opinion, they in fact represent only private or mass opinion: opinion taken in the dark of the doorway rather than in the light of the forum; opinion that chokes off the opportunity to hear out arguments pro and con, to consult a neighbour, to read up, to ask a question, to answer back; opinion so half-hearted it is hard to take seriously.

If I vote in an election or referendum I must come away from my house – a small act perhaps but enough to underscore a responsibility and commitment. But if I answer an opinion poll questionnaire my commitment, if there is commitment at all, is likely to be trivialised to the level of a preference for a brand of pears or suntan lotions – which is in fact the actual context of most opinion polls, as they are tacked-on questions to consumer surveys.

Not many, to be sure, would go along with the proposal of George Gallup that opinion polls take the place of free elections.

But can the opinion polls give a reasonably accurate reading of grass roots opinion? In even the best-conducted opinion poll there is no way to be so much as half way sure about so basic a question as what the subject is about. An opinion poll among Glasgow council tenants in high rise flats showed 91 per cent of them satisfied. Puzzled by such astonishing contentment, sociologist Pearl Jephcott personally interviewed council tenants. She found that what residents meant by satisfaction was that they had a roof over their heads that didn't leak, or that they were glad to get out from their in-laws or find a flat they could afford, or simply that they were self-respecting and respectable. As for high rise flats, no, these were dreadful. An opinion poll on satisfaction has a special methodological problem: satisfaction is such a powerful vacuum cleaner it sucks up satisfaction from unrelated sources and tends to give a bloated score.

By a popular misuse of the term, an opinion poll is synonymous with any short survey. It is not. A survey asking how you would vote if there were an election tomorrow is a poll about voting intention. Unlike the opinion poll, you can check its performance by its eve of election forecast. But you cannot check the performance of an opinion poll – a point which is conveniently forgotten when the two types of polls are bracketed together.

Nor is an opinion poll like a brief attitude survey that asks, say, whether you are more worried about inflation than you are about unemployment. This short survey can also suffer distortions but the risk is considerably less. The subject of the question is likely to be decipherable; so is the answer. After all, we know more about our worries than we do about secondary picketing.

Nor is an opinion poll like the brief survey of leaders and issues used by political parties during election campaigns. Here the technique is much the same as a conventional opinion poll but the purpose is radically different. The political party isn't trying to discover a mandate but simply to check its own communication. Has a message been received, is it convincing, which issues and leadership characteristics appeal most to which target groups – these are the practical questions asked by political communication surveys. These questions are entirely legitimate.

The British Road Federation once devised a poll to show that Londoners wanted more urban motorways. Cooking the results was easy enough. The poll had only to ask a yes/no question. Respondents were thus forced to choose between getting something they could conceivably enjoy and getting nothing at all. Peter Willmott and Michael Young stepped in on the side of the angels and launched an opinion poll of their own. This poll offered alternative forms of government expenditure. Lo, help for the elderly came first while more urban motorways came last.

Willmott and Young fell for the temptation of reform. Indeed they fell so hard they quite forgot research protocol. They had neglected to rotate the list of alternatives. More help for the elderly was in the first position – and the first position, like the second least expensive wine, is known to be favoured. They had also stacked the cards against urban motorways by offering three types of transport expenditure but only one for the social services and housing – tantamount to forcing Tories to split their vote by fielding three candidates per constituency.

A survey on tinned pears or suntan lotion will take 35–40 minutes; yet a widely publicised poll on realignments in British politics may take four or five minutes. Why must we figleaf the true character of an opinion poll? It is often only another name for a cheapjack survey. And it shows.

Adapted from *New Statesman* 6 February 1981

1 What differences are there between opinion polls and:
a short surveys?
b the methods used by political parties during an election?
c brief attitude surveys?

2 Explain why the following are important in getting an accurate survey of people's opinions:
a careful use of words like 'satisfied';
b the order in which questions are asked;
c the way alternative answers are arranged;
d the way surveys use yes/no answers.

3 Would you agree with George Gallup (an American who started one of the first opinion polls) that opinion polls should take the place of free elections? Give reasons for your answer.

47

People power

How can ordinary people put pressure on local government to gain some control of what is done to the community? Tony Gibson describes the way a group of people in Carlisle took on their local council.

Mrs Betty Dunham has lived all her life in a big Victorian house with a double staircase, overlooking a small garden square in the middle of Carlisle. Her husband was a seafarer; they did not have a great social life; what there was revolved around church work, committee work for the Lifeboat Institution, and the ward Conservative Party.

When she heard a rumour that the Council were building a radial road through the square, she wrote to them and asked if it was true. They wrote back and said there was nothing in it, but if ever it was mooted she would be informed.

The next thing was that she read in the paper that a meeting of the Highways Planning Committee had decided not to go through the square 'at this stage'. The mere fact that 'they were already harbouring the thought of going through after having said they wouldn't, that made me absolutely livid'. She badgered the Civil Centre until she eventually got her interview with the City Engineer, and afterwards had a council of war with her neighbour, Mr Blenkiron, whom she had taken with her. (Mr Blenkiron chaired the Gardens Committee of the little square, which met once a year to keep an eye on the behaviour of residents' pets, and see that the flower beds were in good order.)

Mr Blenkiron agreed that it was time 'to have a little meeting, just of the local people, down in the church hall'. He thought it would be a pity to confine it to the Gardens Committee. So Mrs Dunham mentioned it to Mrs Powell next door, and Mr Powell, who had an allotment, mentioned it to the chairman of the allotments. Mrs Powell saw a rather good letter in the local paper from a Mr Pitt, who lived nearby, so she rang him; he rang Mr Barnes who was a friend of his. Mrs Dunham also went round to see the Christian Science church, and local nunnery, and chatted up everyone she knew in the neighbourhood and several more that she hadn't even been introduced to.

The meeting at the church hall was packed. Mrs Dunham said her piece about cars being all right if they are kept within reason and a rotten ride being better than a good walk, but that didn't mean the cars should come belting through poisoning everybody with their fumes all the time, and spoiling the houses and taking people away from their environments. Nearly everyone else present had their say too, 'and when we all had had our little say, we decided that we would have an "action committee", for want of a better word'.

Mr Blenkiron already had enough on his plate, and some others who were proposed were reluctant to stand, Mr Barnes had spoken very well, so somebody proposed him and he was made the chairman. Anyone else who wanted to be on the committee was invited to join it. Before the meeting broke up the committee had got to know each other and decided on the first steps to be taken.

They leafletted and flyposted the district, and booked the city hall hoping that with luck they would get fifty people along. It was filled to bursting, with over 600 inside and 200 turned away. The City Preservation Society was formed on the spot, the committee re-elected, funds raised, and a series of confrontations began to take place, on television, radio, and in the council's offices, all designed to extract information, street by street and area by area, on what was being planned.

At least half the committee was made up of people like Eric Scott, a milk roundsman who knew everyone in his manor, kept a fatherly eye on potential young vandals, gave a helping hand to pensioners living on their own, and was not afraid of a dust-up whenever it proved necessary. At first, he said, he was doubtful whether he and his mates could keep their end up with what he called 'the hoity toities' from the garden square: people who were very good at holding coffee mornings to spread the word, and laying down the law to council officials. But he concluded that in his own way he knew just as much what mattered; on his rounds he was in touch with every householder, knew their reactions to every move that was being made, and could spot a lurking surveyor even before he got out his tape measure.

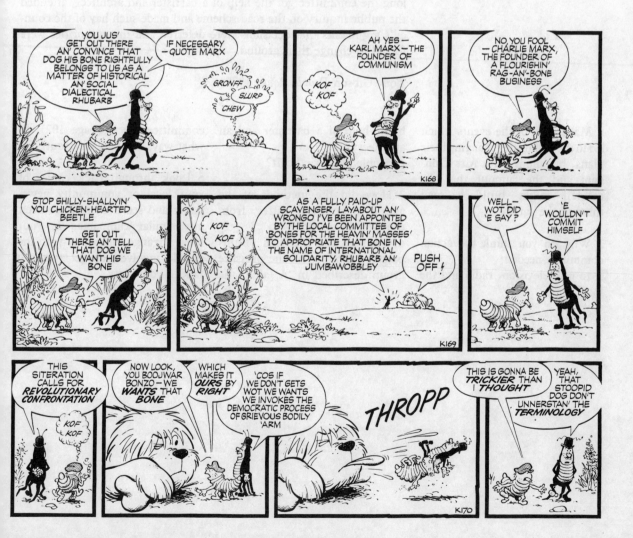

115

Mr Scott has voted Labour in his time, but says the way the council are behaving he's inclined to vote Conservative. Jim Barnes, who is a teacher in a school for handicapped children, is a Communist. Mrs Dunham (Conservative) says, 'I don't give a hoot what his politics is. He's an excellent chairman – very fair. I couldn't care less if Stalin was his uncle.'

The group involved everyone within reach, by door-to-door contact, then small local meetings, leading to bigger meetings, securing more publicity locally and nationally in the press and on radio and television, arousing the professional interests of architects and planners, getting their help and advice, and so giving a professional exposure of the situation in local conferences and national journals.

In contrast the council had been accustomed to rationing the information, to limiting opportunities for outsiders to find out what was going on, to reaching crucial decisions behind closed doors. The publicity obtained by the action group gave it leverage, gradually opening up the situation so that the whole community took an interest. Before long the committee got the help of a barrister and architect, attended the public inquiry on the road scheme and made such hay of the council's arguments that decisions were deferred and the authorities were forced to change their ground.

Tony Gibson *People Power* 1979

1 Make a list of the events which led to the authorities changing their plans, beginning with Mrs Dunham and the rumour that the council might build a road through the square.

2 Why do you think the action committee needed:
a to use television, radio and the local press;
b the help of a barrister and an architect;
c people like Eric Scott?

3 How did the methods of the action committee differ from those of the council?
4 Compare the methods of this pressure group with the pressure group described in 'A fall at the committee fence' (page 102). In what ways are they different?

5 Look through back copies of your local or community newspaper and see if there have been any similar campaigns in your area. Arrange interviews with the people involved or get them to talk to your class.

48
The working class Tory

A number of explanations have been given for working class Conservative voting. In this account of voting in Salford at the beginning of the twentieth century Robert Roberts gives examples of pragmatic and deference patterns of voting. Pragmatic voting occurs when the voters expect the party of their choice to do something which will be to their advantage. Deference voters choose a party because they believe that it is made up of the natural leaders who have a right to expect their vote.

Our district voted solidly Conservative except for once in the famous election of 1906, when a fear that the Tories' tariff reform policy might increase the price of food alarmed the humble voter. A Conservative victory, it was widely bruited, would mean the 'little loaf', a Liberal win, the 'big loaf'. These were politics the poor could understand! They threw out the local brewer, their long-standing representative, in favour of a Liberal. Men like my father, who revered Lloyd George, free-trade-minded shopkeepers and the few artisans around were delighted – until the next election! The overwhelming majority of unskilled workers remained politically illiterate still. The less they had to conserve the more conservative in spirit they showed themselves. Wages paid and hours worked might spark off discussion at the pub and street corner, but such things were often talked of like the seasons – as if no one could expect to have any influence on their vagaries. Many were genuinely grateful to an employer for being kind enough to use their services at all. Voting Conservative, they felt at one with him. It was their belief, widely expressed at election times, that the middle and upper classes with their better intelligence and education had a natural right to think and act on behalf of the rest, a right that one should not even question. In Bristol as late as 1909 there were only eight Labour representatives on a council of ninety-two. In all, then, before 1914 it is true to say that a poor man knew his place: he wanted that place recognised, however humble, and he required others to keep theirs. To command his class respect, it needed to be shown by means of money, mien, goods or connections that one belonged to a higher social level. Then, and only then, as a free-standing Englishman, would he doff his cap. Apathy, docility, deference: our village as a whole displayed just those qualities which, sixty years before, Karl Marx had noted, stamped the poor industrial workers – qualities which convinced him that the English proletarian would never revolt of his own accord.

Robert Roberts *The Classic Slum* 1971

1 How did the election of 1906 show evidence of 'pragmatic' voting?

2 Why did the working class of Salford believe that the Conservatives would make better rulers?

3 What did Marx see as the characteristics of English workers?

49
Beware the county crackdown

There are 135 main ways a motorist can fall foul of the law in Britain. But his or her chances of getting caught for a particular offence can depend on what part of the country he or she is in. So where are the hotspots – and for which offences? And why the anomalies?

If a motorist jumps the lights in Manchester, he seems to run more risk of being booked than if he drives the 68 miles to Sheffield and tries his luck there.

That's because Manchester, which with Salford has about as many miles of roads as Sheffield and its twin authority, Rotherham, notched up 1450 convictions against Sheffield's 129.

On the other hand, Sheffield cracks down more often on drivers with defective tyres. In 1972, the police prosecuted 1584 of them for this offence – nearly 500 more than were prosecuted 77 miles away in Birmingham, with 800 miles more roads and twice as large a police force.

On that basis, the best place to 'burn old socks' is in Northumberland, where in 1972 only four motorists were prosecuted for having dirty exhaust emissions. But in Hertfordshire, which has about 800 fewer miles of road, the police prosecuted 245 motorists for this offence and issued 72 written warnings.

Although the statistics must be viewed in the light of police strength, comparative miles of roads, local vehicle registration, population figures, or even in the number of traffic lights where relevant, different constabularies do appear to have more success with some misdemeanours than with others.

There is certainly no national pattern of prosecution among the 47 police authorities in England and Wales.

Take Derbyshire. With just over 3000 miles of road the police prosecuted only 62 motorists with faulty silencers and gave only five warnings in writing.

Compare that to Hertfordshire police who appear to be so hot on the trail of the noisy vehicle on their 2500-odd miles of road that they prosecuted 574 culprits, and issued written warnings to 90.

True enough, Derbyshire, being a rural area, can be expected to attract a much smaller volume of traffic than a Home County like Hertfordshire, but that in itself surely doesn't explain such a wide gap in the prosecution figures.

Hertfordshire's chief constable, Mr Raymond Buxton, who is secretary of the Traffic Committee of the Association of Chief Police Officers, says, 'I do agree that in the latest statistical returns, there are a number of apparent disparities between police forces.

'These occur from year to year and, while in some instances the pattern remains fairly constant, in other cases changes occur without explanation.'

But who shall be prosecuted, and for what offence, often depends on the directives sent out by individual chief constables, and their policy decisions can be influenced by many surprising factors.

As one senior metropolitan police officer says: 'If parents complain that their children cannot cross a particular road in safety the Chief

Constable might order a radar meter to be used for a week. Prosecutions for speeding then jump up; drivers get the message – and for the time being the parents are pacified.'

Commander Gordon Maggs, head of the Metropolitan Police traffic division, says: 'We could prosecute 1000 motorists daily for speeding, but what is the point? Unless there is a direct link between the accident rate on a particular road and the speeds at which vehicles are travelling we don't put radar meters into operation.'

This attitude is reflected in the Metropolitan Police's tally of speeding prosecutions in 1972. In that year the force prosecuted about 9000 fewer speeders than Lancashire Constabulary, which is some 300 men short and has 1600 fewer miles of road to police.

'We are not here to persecute drivers, but it is our job to enforce the law, keep down accidents and save lives,' said a Lancashire police spokesman.

It is how this philosophy is interpreted that governs the attitude of a police force towards the traffic offender.

Other unconnected and even mundane happenings like a political demonstration, or an outbreak of farm disease, can reduce a motorist's vulnerability to prosecution. A council chamber rumpus over accident figures can lead to extra police activity towards drivers in one district. But while these are valid contributory causes, they are not in themselves enough to explain the more glaring anomalies.

In Essex, for instance, there was one prosecution for defective tyres for nearly every mile of road in 1972, and over twice as many for speeding. The police, however, only summoned a meagre 123 motorists for lighting infringements. (Bedfordshire, with 1250 miles of road to police, collected more than 2500 lighting offenders in the same calendar period.)

"*Notice how he undoes his scarf before giving **his** version of what happened.*"

Mr J. Duke, Acting Chief Constable of Essex and Southend Constabulary, explains: 'In 1972, in my police area, there were 19 fatal accidents, and 220 serious and 224 slight injury accidents where speeding was regarded as a contributory cause. It follows that our vigilance on this offence has good reason.

'It is true we are relatively low in the lighting offence table. One answer may be that verbal warnings are given providing the fault concerned is immediately rectified.'

Although the general efficiency of his force will be inspected by HM Inspector of Constabulary, it is the Chief Constable who has the final responsibility for deciding which traffic offences will be prosecuted most vigorously.

Over one and a quarter million motorists were prosecuted for motoring offences in 1972. Almost certainly justifiably prosecuted in most cases – except that for many there will be the feeling they had the ill-luck to be in the wrong police area at the time of the offence.

Harry Loftus *Drive Magazine* 1974

1 What explanations might be given for different levels of prosecution by the police in different parts of the country?

2 How might the action of a member of the public lead to an increase in prosecutions?

3 What events might lead to an increase in the number of prosecutions for the following offences?
a speeding
b defective tyres
c burglary
d drunken driving
e mugging
f fraud

4 Explain why you would agree or disagree with the view that 'statistics of police convictions are an accurate reflection of the number of offences committed.'

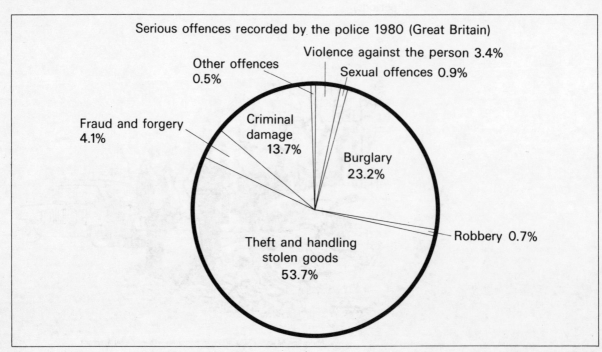

Serious offences recorded by the police 1980 (Great Britain)

Other offences 0.5%

Violence against the person 3.4%

Sexual offences 0.9%

Fraud and forgery 4.1%

Criminal damage 13.7%

Burglary 23.2%

Robbery 0.7%

Theft and handling stolen goods 53.7%

Source: *Social Trends*

50
The organisation of thieving

We often read in newspapers of the 'professional criminal'. Mary McIntosh suggests that crime may be seen as a profession like any other. The traditional 'craft' thief has, she suggests, been replaced by the more highly organised 'project thief'.

In the very simplest societies there are no professional criminals. In these, as in any society, if there are laws people commit crimes; if there is property people steal from each other; but no one makes his living by stealing from others. It is only in more complex societies that crime emerges as a full-time occupation for some people and it becomes possible to distinguish between these – the professional criminals – and the amateur or casual criminals and delinquents. Professional criminals can then be studied like any other occupational group, we can study not only why people take up this occupation, as criminologists have traditionally done, but also how the occupational tasks are divided up and interrelated, how working groups and occupational communities with hierarchies of status and of authority are formed, and what the relations between these groups and communities and other groups are like. We can study the social organisation of professional crime because it is a socially ordered activity. Professional criminals follow the rules and customs of their work much as other workers do. It is said that there is 'honour among thieves'; in fact the mutual expectations among criminals go far beyond mere honour, and cover all the understandings and agreements necessary to their cooperative activity. The seeming paradox of a willingness to disobey some of the rules of the state and yet to abide by the customs of their own group is an everyday reality for criminals.

However, to say that crime can be studied like any other social activity is not to say that it *is* exactly like any other social activity. Crime is a special form of deviant behaviour; and deviant behaviour is a form of conflict behaviour – because it is defined as behaviour that most people, or the most powerful people, disapprove of and try to stop. Crime is that deviant behaviour which is forbidden by law. In societies with a state this means that the criminal is in conflict with the state and its agencies of law enforcement, as well as with any people he may be injuring, such as property owners and insurance companies.

Craft criminals aim not to be noticed while they are working, even though their victims may be present at the time. Indeed, many a craft theft is never discovered at all since it is hard to know whether things have been lost or stolen. This is the major way in which craft criminals reduce the risks of detection. Project criminals, on the other hand, often risk recognition or retaliation by facing their victims and letting them know they are being robbed. The hold-up is the clearest example of this: bank robbers traditionally announce, 'This is a hold up.' Though they must run such risks if they are to undertake the projects at all, they always try to reduce them as much as possible. To reduce the risk of being identified they often wear masks, spectacles, false moustaches or uniform clothing bought specially for the occasion. To reduce the risk of retaliation or of an alarm being sounded one or more of the team may carry a gun and tell those present to stand still or to raise their hands.

Because of the advanced and changing technology and because of the relatively small number of really attractive collections of money or valuables, each project theft, or short series of thefts, presents its own unique problems. Each job may therefore require a different assortment of somewhat specialised skills, one calling for an expert in alarm systems, another for a driver of a getaway car, one for a safecracker, another for a strong arm man. Typically, therefore, project thefts are carried out by an *ad hoc* team of men chosen and coordinated for a particular job rather than by a gang who work regularly together.

The picture is rather reminiscent of the way in which a small builder and decorator gathers together a team including plumbers and electricians to carry out a house conversion.

Mary McIntosh *Changes in the Organisation of Thieving* 1971

1 Why is crime a 'special form of deviant behaviour'. What is it that makes certain kinds of behaviour 'criminal'?

2 With whom is the criminal in conflict?

3 Which of the following criminal activities are more likely to be (1) craft theft or (2) project thefts?
a pickpockets
b bank robbery
c confidence tricks

d housebreaking
e wages snatch

4 Why does project theft need more organisation and teamwork?

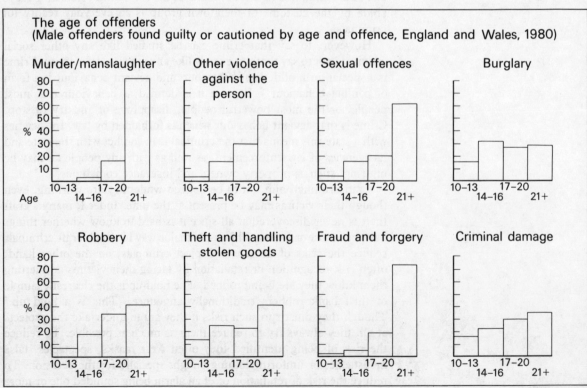

The age of offenders
(Male offenders found guilty or cautioned by age and offence, England and Wales, 1980)

Source: *Social Trends*

51
On the fiddle

Crime may take many forms and some crimes are thought to be more serious than others. Many people would not even think that taking things from your employer or 'making a bit on the side' are criminal. Jason Ditton studied the way bread delivery men added to their wages by regular fiddling:

In its simplest form, 'fiddling' is overcharging. The salesman regularly overcharges the customer. The first stage of the fiddle ('making' money) exploits the driver's relationship with the customer, with the talent and poise of the conman. The second stage ('taking' the profit) is engineered with the delicate positional cover of the embezzler. The 'fiddle' is normally disguised as a legitimate sales activity which provides protection for the fiddler and satisfaction for the consumer.

Briefly, a 'fiddle' is a theft by a service agent from his customer which is practised in such a way as to make it invisible. Theft from the firm by a salesman is either 'stealing', when openly individualistic, or 'dealing' when it also involves the subversion of other employees. The bakery management makes a crucial distinction between 'fiddling' (which they encourage) and 'stealing' and 'dealing' (which they make periodic attempts to stamp out). The managerial attitude is reflected in their treatment of those caught out. When I asked a sales supervisor why men were sacked for 'fiddling', he said:

> Who? Who gets fired for fiddling then? I've never known anybody get fired for fiddling since I've been here. . .can you name anybody? [I did] . . . Ah!, he wasn't caught for fiddling, was he? He was stealing . . . I know it sounds funny . . . (but) they don't care what you do in shops, as long as the sales are OK, and you don't come short . . . That bloke [that I had mentioned] was taking it from despatch, and that's an entirely different thing.

Salesmen occasionally find that they can fiddle with the full knowledge, and even cooperation, of the customer! For example, one salesman said:

> 'Some of them don't care, one of my customers told me this summer that he had to add so much on to one of this customer's bills to cover what I fiddle him. . .so he obviously knew I was fiddling him, but he wasn't bothered, he passes the fiddle on.'

Whilst they officially condemn personal theft, the management expect the men to pass a final 'test' of directing some of the 'made' money to their own pockets. As the sales manager regularly says, 'They're not real salesmen if they can't make a bob or two on the side, are they?' Although the management are relatively sympathetic towards 'personal' fiddling such as this, at the same time they fear that open encouragement from them would lead the men to become attached to crime and thus steal from the company, or 'deal' with some of its more unscrupulous inside employees. But teaching the men to fiddle does carry the seeds of its own destruction in precisely this way. Right from the start, roundsmen see double standards. One said, 'They seem to think that taking bread from them is wrong, and fiddling their customers is right.' A supervisor, who used to introduce the fiddle as a joke in training, realised that for most of the men: 'It's probably in the back of their minds "I can do that for myself and make a few shillings".' Occasionally, supervisors overtly suggest that the new man should 'take a dip in the bag', at least to cover those financial needs (cigarettes, tea) occurring during the day's work. One roundsman remembered that, 'He told me I should do it to cover myself, just for a packet of fags', and another recalled, 'He was also saying I should pocket it, whatever I could make. . .he didn't say any specific amount.'

As the roundsman practises by himself, he will mix more with the other salesmen than with the supervisors. He will eat less of the goods, make fewer mistakes and begin to build up trust with his customers. Importantly, he will develop sleight of hand at fiddling generally, and specifically learn the 'easy touches' on his route. The likelihood of him continuing to come short on his weekly money decreases just at the same time as his skills at fiddling improve.

'You can't get away with anything. . .when you first start off. . .they're all a bit wary of you. . .but after a bit they trust you, and you can start fiddling them more and more.
'After a bit you've got the ones what add up what they had, and the ones that didn't . . . I used to try them out . . . I used to think 'Oh! I'll put threepence on, and see if she says anything'. . .if the bill was four and sixpence, I used to say: "That'll be four and nine, please ma'am" and if she didn't say anything about it, I'd know she didn't add up. . .put a penny on this, put a penny on that, you try it, then you think "Oh well, that's two or three pounds extra in my pocket". . .that used to worry me at first. . .but it isn't pennies now, it's pounds.'

Jason Ditton *Part-time Crime* 1977

1 What is the difference between
a fiddling
b stealing
c dealing?
Which of these is considered to be a crime?

2 What is the attitude of (a) the management, (b) the customers, towards fiddling?

3 How does the delivery man learn to fiddle?

4 What are the similarities and differences between
a shoplifting
b confidence tricks
c mugging
d fraud?

52
Comics

What effect do comics have on the way young children learn to see the world and their place in it? Sue Sharpe suggests that they have an influence on the development of masculine and feminine roles.

One of the nicest things I remember doing as a child, especially on rainy days, or during long school holidays, was lying on the floor reading comics. They seemed very innocent then, but looking back and reviewing them today, it is clear that they endorse the same roles and images as children's books and readers. From the simple picture strip papers, to pop and love stories and the glossy magazines, the portrayal of girls and their concerns and interests is narrow and circumscribed.

For very young children who are just beginning to read, there are girls' comics like *Twinkle* ('The picture paper especially for little girls') and others for both sexes like *Jack and Jill*, *Playhour* and *Robin*. In *Twinkle*, little girls are shown doing various activities, but many of the stories have a similar theme, involving the familiar stereotypes. One recurring theme is that of helping people and doing good turns. 'Babs the Brownie' learns 'Kim game' (remembering lots of items that have been shown for a minute or so) – which turns out to be extremely useful when her mother forgets her shopping list the next day. Goldilocks gets her three bears to perform for the little girl in hospital who could not go to the circus. Patty Pickle wants to help her mother with the housework, but she is so clumsy and inefficient that she is set to clear her doll's house instead. I'm sure it wouldn't happen to Peter Pickle! Familiar roles are seen in 'Nancy the Little Nurse', who mends the broken dollies in the dollies' hospital with her grandad, who is the dolly doctor. Apart from mummy, who is either doing housework, or taking her daughter walking and to the shops, adults rarely enter the scene. The comics for both boys and girls are marginally better, if only because they often feature animals instead of children, like 'Harold the Hare' and 'Fliptail the Otter' who engage in slightly more activities that are neutral and less sex biased, although the animals are still given a gender and often act accordingly. When children do enter, however, the same themes occur like 'Nurse Susan and Doctor David', a 'let's pretend' story.

For children of seven or eight, up to about thirteen years of age, comics are divided sharply into those for boys and those for girls. Girls read *Bunty*, *Judy*, *June* and *Mandy*, among others, all titles taking the form of a girl's name. Boys read comics with names like *Victor*, *Valiant*, *Hotspur*, *Lion*, *Thunder* and *Hornet* – names which embody virile masculine associations. The differences in the style of the titles implies and reflects the orientations of the contents. The majority of boys' stories are action packed adventures, taking place in wild and remote lands on spaceships or other planets, or on football pitches and racetracks. Physical feats are performed against inestimable odds; contests and conflicts, battles, tests of skill and ingenuity pour continuously out of every page. Stories are loud and noisy – VROOSH! SKREECH! CRUUUSH! BAAANG! VROOM! AAAARGH! ricochet round the pages.

Girls' comics conspicuously lack this sort of action. Stories tend to involve coping with unexpected situations, or taking part in individual competitions, trying to prove the innocence of someone wrongly accused, or helping people to rediscover their lost families. Almost every story seems to contain some personal or emotional element. Heroines have to be able to inspire sympathy in the reader for what they are fighting for, or against, in order to be recognised in all their true worthiness. Personalities are laid out in much more detail than in stories for boys. Much more care is taken to show either the sincerity or the wickedness of the characters. Because the hopes and beliefs of the heroine are so fully set out, it is much easier to identify with her, in her vulnerable and exposed moments. In all these stories the message comes across that it is girls alone who are sensitive enough both to have feelings themselves and to be able to detect them in others.

Backgrounds to girls' comic stories are much narrower in range than those for boys. Male action can take place in any part of this, or indeed, any other world. But for girls, most stories are based in the home, the family or the school, which also therefore provide the main restricting authorities. The action, potentially defined by the background, is restricted from the start. It has been claimed that girls' comic stories benefit from having more 'realistic' elements in them and that this is better than the extreme fantasy found in boys' comics. However, all imaginations, regardless of sex, need to be, and enjoy being, kindled, and fantastic action is probably more creative and exciting than the slower more 'inward directed' stories that are presented to girls. Since background confines characters, it is significant that most of the boys' heroes are adult men – soldiers, spacemen, cowboys, footballers and scientists. They don't have restricting families. They can go where they like and do what they want. None of them are married. By comparison, the chief characters produced for girls are usually in their teens. Their families have to be accounted for somehow and often large parts of a story are devoted to the problem of coping with a family or with trying to survive without one. In stories where parents play a major role, they are usually in some difficulty and the daughter comes to the rescue.

Sue Sharpe *Just Like a Girl* 1976

1 Describe the main features of comics for:
a very young girls;
b very young boys and girls;
c girls aged 7–13;
d boys aged 7–13.

2 In your own words describe:
a the typical female character who appears in comics;
b the typical male character in comics.

3 Collect comics in each of the main groups above and examine the extent to which they confirm Sue Sharpe's viewpoint.

53

The trials of Miss Snobby Snout

'Jackie Stanton won £2,000 in an essay competition – and bought her family's council house on the Sawbridge estate. But no one else on the estate owned their own house – and the Stantons became the target for increasing hostility.' So begins a recent episode of 'The house that Jackie bought', a regular feature in *Tracy*, a weekly comic for girls produced by the Dundee-based DC Thomson organisation.

The saga started in April, when the Stantons were friendly with all their neighbours but Jackie's widowed mother was in rent arrears because of a five week lay off at the factory where she worked. Thirteen year old Jackie is appalled by the prospect of a transfer to 'grotty old Coniston Blocks, where the problem families live' and when she wins her £2,000 she decides to purchase the family's council house – receiving a hefty discount because of their fifteen year tenancy. Since then life has been hard for the Stantons.

Jackie ('Miss Toffee Nose') is harassed and upset by some animal-like louts from the Coniston Blocks who appear to spend their entire time (when not victimising Jackie) lounging on a wrecked car and running a pensioner protection racket. She is insulted by her classmates, plagued by a rat and framed for stealing a pair of tights from a local supermarket. Her sister is rejected by her best friend and – under threat of blackmail – driven to sleepwalking and trying to smash and grab some sweets. Her brother has lost all his friends and is assaulted by a neighbouring parent. As homeowners the Stantons are excluded from the regular seaside outing, and the neighbours turn against them after they erect a sign saying 'Our House'. A few weeks ago Jackie was hit by a car while trying to escape from a gang of hooded local tearaways; while recovering in hospital she is sent a chocolate box full of worms addressed to 'Miss Snobby Snout'.

The Stantons are well dressed, well spoken and pretty. Practically every council tenant that appears is brutish or haggard and inclined to speak in non-BBC style. The motives behind the hate campaign are simply that the Stantons are homeowners and their opponents are tenants.

R. Edwards *New Statesman* 1980

1 The mass media convey political as well as social messages. What messages are conveyed in the comic story 'The trials of Miss Snobby Snout'? Why do you think these might be considered to be 'political' messages?

2 This is an extract which uses stereotypes. (See 'Man in the street'). Describe the stereotypes that are used in this passage.

3 In real life the things which happen to Jackie Stanton would be examples of stigmatisation. When individuals or groups are separated out and treated differently because others feel that they are in some way 'different', sociologists say that they are being 'stigmatised'. Make a list of other examples of stigmatisation.

54
Processing the news

In examining how news gets into a newspaper Jeremy Tunstall uses the concept of the 'gatekeeper' who only permits certain news to pass through his 'gate'. A newsroom on a national daily paper has a number of 'gatekeepers' at different stages in the process.

The usual physical arrangement of the nightdesk is a 'backbench' – such senior processors as the night editor, deputy night editor and chief subeditor – facing two or more long tables of subeditors. Much of the work must be done in about three hours. During this intensive period no one man can read all the words which will constitute the first edition of a daily newspaper. Large quantities of material will be rejected – or 'spiked' – so total reading is even more impossible. Further, the processors do not merely read but also cut, rewrite, update stories with new matter, check spellings and write headlines. There is some division of labour: firstly, by pages – front, sports, features, etc.: secondly, processors specialise according to the stage in the flow. Some processors gatekeep for others farther on in the flow. After the copy has left the newdesk it will be 'copytasted'; if not rejected, it then goes to an executive (e.g. deputy night editor) who will give it a 'catchline' (preliminary title) and a rough indication of the number of words required; a subeditor then does the detailed processing. The processed story is next returned to the backbench where, if accepted and of suitable size, it will be allotted perhaps half a column on page 3 by an executive – say, the chief subeditor – who is 'laying out' this page. Later still, yet another gatekeeper, a 'stone subeditor', with proof in hand and the story set in the composing room, may make another cut. So, after leaving the newsdesk the piece of copy passes perhaps five or six gatekeepers before reaching print.

Such specialisation of gatekeepers at different stages in the flow (and at different hierarchical levels) contrasts with newsgathering, where specialisation is primarily by subject-matter. A senior gatherer will deal with just one subject, but a senior processor may deal with all the 'inside' news pages – for which he will select 'page leads' from political, crime, human interest, aviation, beauty queen, animal, and other stories. Processors must also consider appearance. Within a very few minutes a chief processor will (in consultation with his picture editor) select a picture of a photogenic kitten, while throwing a pile of glossy dog, panda and pony pictures on the floor; next he selects one girl who provides the best combination of leg quality and photographic quality, while other assorted starlets and débutantes join the ponies and pandas on the floor; then he interrogates the office lawyer about possible libel in a crime story; next on to a late-arriving United Nations story.

Pages are made up around advertisements, with pictures and headlines especially affected. Using blue pencil, scissors and paste, processors must rapidly butcher copy upon which other men and women have spent their whole day. There is some specialisation by subjects (e.g. sport), but much less than in gathering; newspapers like the *Daily Express* and *Daily Mirror* which had substantial staffs of foreign correspondents nevertheless process their foreign and domestic news together. The 'splash' subeditor processes the front page lead story regardless of its subject. A story is assigned to a subeditor primarily according to its importance and to his seniority 'up the table' (that is physically closer to the backbench).

The gatekeeping role of copy tasters includes regulating the total flow to the processing executive – according to space available at the time and date (which depends on the amount of advertising, the number of pages for that day's paper and whether it is a busy or slack day for news). Further on in the processing flow is the 'revise' subeditor or 'prodnose', who reads proofs, and checks for matters of house style, policy or inconsistencies between stories.

As each edition time approaches, the processing team works at great speed and pressure. If a reporter hands his copy in at the newsdesk, but does not see it in the paper next morning, all he will know is that it disappeared somewhere in the processing process.

Jeremy Tunstall *Journalists at Work* 1971

1 How many 'gatekeepers' are involved in the stages which a news item must pass through between leaving the 'newsdesk' and getting into print.

2 What is meant by:
a 'spiking'
b 'a catchline'
c 'laying out'
d 'page leads'
e 'the splash'
f 'prodnose'
g 'copy tasting'?

3 Who has the greatest power over what gets into print: gatherers or processors?

4 To what extent is producing a newspaper similar to any other production process, such as making motor cars or washing machines?

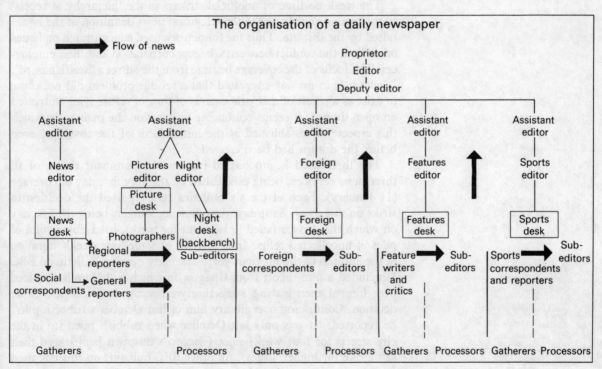

The organisation of a daily newspaper

55

And now, rubbish

Newspaper and television do not just present news, they organise it and interpret it. Often they give a view of the news which does not always agree with what actually happened. The Glasgow Media Group examined how television reported the 1975 Glasgow drivers' strike.

The framework, used by television journalists in reporting disputes, is to employ limited aspects of a dispute to create a dominant view. A strike has its roots in grievances or demands but it also has human protagonists and visible results and ramifications. All of this, as in the events in Glasgow, is 'news'.

'The Glasgow rubbish' or the 'Glasgow rubbish strike' was one of the biggest stories featured in the bulletins during the recording period, covered in 102 bulletins over three months from 11 January to 14 April 1975. As regards the coverage given, it could be seen as one of the most important television news stories of the first half of the year. The heavy goods vehicle (HGV) licence holders, working for Glasgow corporation (over half of them drivers of dustcarts), went on strike. The most public result of this action was that the uncollected refuse was eventually partially cleared by the army. This was the first time in some 25 years that troops had been used in an industrial dispute.

The coverage began with the strike decision and continued periodically as new angles were highlighted until the drivers returned to work on 14 April. The dispute was treated by the Glasgow corporation and the government as a matter of extreme importance. Yet despite the extensive national television coverage of the issues raised, the actual case of the men on strike was neglected.

The weak position of unofficial strikers in the 'hierarchy of access' to the media contributed to the television news definition of the issues raised by the dispute. Thus the framework used concentrated on issues other than the conflict between Glasgow corporation and their employees. The focus of the coverage became from the outset a 'health hazard'. Whilst it is in no way suggested that a serious problem did not come to exist as a result of many thousands of tons of refuse lying untreated on open dumps, it seems reasonable to question the manner in which this aspect was established as the initial focus of the coverage, even before the dumps had been created.

The threatened health hazard became the dominant theme of all three news services, being established on the very first day of coverage (11 January). Each of the six bulletins that reported the decision to strike on this day (a Saturday, the following Monday being the first day on which the drivers failed to turn out for work), used library film of piles of uncollected refuse from a strike of some four weeks' duration in the autumn of the previous year. The early evening bulletin on BBC 1 included a film report from Glasgow in which Bill Hamilton voiced over film of men leaving a meeting with some details of the strike decision. Continuing over library film of last October's rubbish piles, he reported: 'It was only last October when rubbish piled up in the city streets for four weeks since Glasgow's dustmen [sic] staged their last strike for higher wages.' All other BBC bulletins on this day used only various cuts of the library footage of autumn's refuse, and in each case the newscaster said that 'the decision to stop work from Monday was bringing fears of a repeat of the situation last October when rubbish piled up in the streets causing a health hazard'. This was seven weeks before 4 March, when Glasgow corporation themselves announced that a health hazard existed.

ITN bulletins, whilst using only their own library film of the October dispute, were not so explicit in suggesting the hazard. 'The strike means that Glasgow faces another pile up of rubbish on the pavements as happened for four weeks last autumn' (newscaster voice-over film; both bulletins identical). ITN's News at Ten on the following day (12 January) repeated the showing of last October's rubbish, as did BBC 1's Nine o'clock News on the 13th. In order to maintain the 'health hazard' angle as the dominant view, this latter bulletin was still for the third day combining the library film of rubbish with the current film, by then available, of parked dustcarts. Emphasis was also placed on the fact that this was the second strike by Glasgow dustcart drivers within three months.

Taking the coverage as a whole, out of 40 bulletins covering the dispute on BBC 1 only four contained reports of the parity claim. Some seven other bulletins contained references to an 'interim offer' or an explanation such as 'over pay', etc. Of a total of 19 reports in BBC 2 bulletins, only two explicitly mention a parity claim. Three others report the issue as 'over pay' and one other 'over a regrading structure'. Of the 43 ITN bulletins, eight report the parity issue and 11 others restrict their reporting of the dispute's cause to simple questions of 'pay', etc. Thus the cause of the dispute is not inevitably reported and, in the minority of cases when it is, most always characterised as being a pay claim with some references to 'parity' and one reference to 'regrading'. The confusion of nomenclature and the lack of reference to the unofficial nature of the dispute has to be added to this assessment of the television coverage of the story.

Glasgow Media Group *Bad News* 1976

1 What was the main 'news angle' of the strike? How far was this an accurate view of what was happening in Glasgow?

2 How did the television news provide visual support for their news angle?

3 On the evidence presented by the Glasgow Media Group do you feel that the television viewer gained a fair view of the events and the issues raised by the strike?

56
Women's magazines

How do magazines present stereotypes of particular groups in society? In particular, how do magazines present a view of women? Carolyn Faulder outlines one approach:

How to get your man and keep him has been the basic message hammered home and home again in every conventional woman's magazine over the last fifty years, and never more so than in the last twenty, when it has suited powerful commercial interests to add their voice and pressure to confirm women in their traditional role of docile homemaker, serene, selfless guardian of the hearth and family.

Home may be a semi in the suburbs or a central city flat at the top of a high rise block, a working girl's bedsitter or a room with your in-laws while you wait to come top of the housing list; it may be a pin-neat terrace house in a town, a mock Georgian detached on a socially ambitious estate or a bungalow on the Costa Geriatrica; maybe it is only a shabby rented flat in a rundown area, or it could be everybody's dream cottage with roses twined round the door.

Homes are everywhere, and wherever they are there is a woman inside cooking and cleaning and sewing and polishing, feeding the baby, minding the toddler, fetching the children from school, washing and ironing her husband's shirts, preparing tasty dishes to reward the breadwinner when he comes home from a hard day's toil, entertaining the boss, coping with difficult teenagers, and so on. Busy, busy, busy all day long with never a moment to question whether this ceaseless domesticity really does equate with being a 'good wife and mother'.

She is perhaps the most familiar stereotype, constantly projected by the advertising in women's magazines, particularly the mass circulation weeklies and monthlies, which then reinforce the image with their complementary editorial content and 'coysy' tone of voice. (I make no apologies for coining an odious word to describe a depressing but far too common type of magazine journalese.) But she is not, of course, the only one. There are many more: the young, trendy, fashion conscious girl, keen on fun and boys; the sophisticated, elegant hostess; the cool, self-assured model; the narcissistic woman, sensually intent on adoring and preserving her looks for her own satisfaction rather than for any lover; and her opposite, the savage seductress out to trap her man by all the feminine wiles in the book. All these types have their magazines, of which there are so many that it would be invidious to name a few titles, even if they are the most obvious examples. But are they appealing to real women, or merely promoting certain images of 'femininity'?

Trevor Millum, analysing the way advertising is used in women's magazines, observes that it does 'act as a moulder of female outlook and does serve as a legitimation of those roles in which so many women find themselves' by constantly and consistently proffering the same roles over and over again for admiration and emulation. Conceivably, this policy could be justified if the roles depicted included *all* the roles peculiar to women's lives, but of course they do not. The independently minded woman, the woman who considers herself an equal to men, the woman who is economically self-sufficient and many other vital, real images of the modern woman in today's society are conspicuous by their absence. Significantly, career advertisements, few in number anyway, tend to be visually drab and unexciting, and are often matched by editorial articles on a limited, safe selection of traditional occupations for women such as secretarial work, nursing, teaching, social work or something in fashion and beauty.

Women's magazines are like those toy kaleidoscopes which you twist so that the same coloured shapes fall into different patterns. Endless variations can be found in the packaging – covers and cover lines, stories, features and problem pages, fashion, beauty and cookery, even the stars – most especially the stars – are all essential ingredients which are skilfully presented to appeal to particular markets. Underlying them all is the basic assumption that a magazine exists to serve its reader primarily in her capacity as a consumer.

Carolyn Faulder *Women's Magazines* 1977

1 How many 'stereotypes' of women are described by Carolyn Faulder? Find examples of these stereotypes in advertisements, magazines and newspapers.

2 Why has it 'suited powerful commercial interests to confirm women in their traditional role of docile homemaker'?

3 Collect examples of women's magazines and measure the amount of space given to:
a homemaking;
b careers;
c aiming to please men;
d politics.

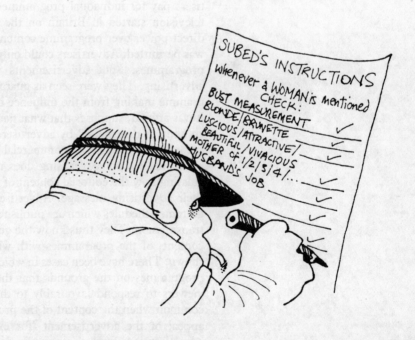

133

57

How the audience is made

What lies behind the way television companies organise their programmes? Is television advertising just a way of financing television entertainment? James Curran and Jean Seaton don't think so.

Commercial television produces audiences not programmes. Advertisers, in purchasing a few seconds of television time, are actually buying viewers by the thousand. The price they pay is determined by the number of people who can be expected to be watching when their advert is shown. Hence advertisers regard programmes merely as the means by which audiences are delivered to them. The sequence of programmes in any evening, week, or season reflects the quest of commercial customers to get the largest or most appropriate public they can. 'The spot is the packaging,' wrote a market researcher in *Advertising Quarterly* (June 1979); 'the product inside the package is an audience.' This determines what kind of programmes are made, when they are shown and who sees them.

The most important pressure on television scheduling is that of advertising expenditure. If television companies sell audiences, what kinds of audience do advertisers want, and how are they packaged to attract sales? Indeed how does the real purpose of producing audiences for advertisers affect the apparent purpose of producing programmes for audience consumption?

The American system of programme sponsorship, in which advertisers pay for individual programmes, was rejected when commercial television started in Britain on the grounds that it gave advertisers direct power over programme content. Instead, only 'spot advertising' was permitted. Advertisers could only buy time slots between or within programmes. Spot advertisements were compared with newspaper advertising. They were seen as guaranteeing the independence of programme making from the influence of advertisers; no rational person, it was argued, supposes that what newspapers publish in their editorial columns is determined by advertisers. Spot advertising would protect the editorial integrity of commercial television.

However, spot advertising does not prevent advertisers from calculating how the editorial content of programmes affects the impact of their advertising message. Advertisers have prior knowledge of programme schedules which are published each quarter in advance of their transmission. They thus know the general character, if not the precise content, of the programmes with which their advertisements will be shown. There have been cases in which advertisers have avoided certain programmes on the grounds that their content is unlikely to dispose viewers to respond favourably to their advertisements. This is most common when the content of the programme clashes directly with the appeal of the advertisement (for example, airlines have withdrawn advertisements from appearing in documentaries about air disasters).

In contrast, some programmes may be preferred because they provide an editorial environment conducive to a favourable response to particular advertisements, or because their prestige is thought likely to enhance that of the product or service advertised within them. Thus,

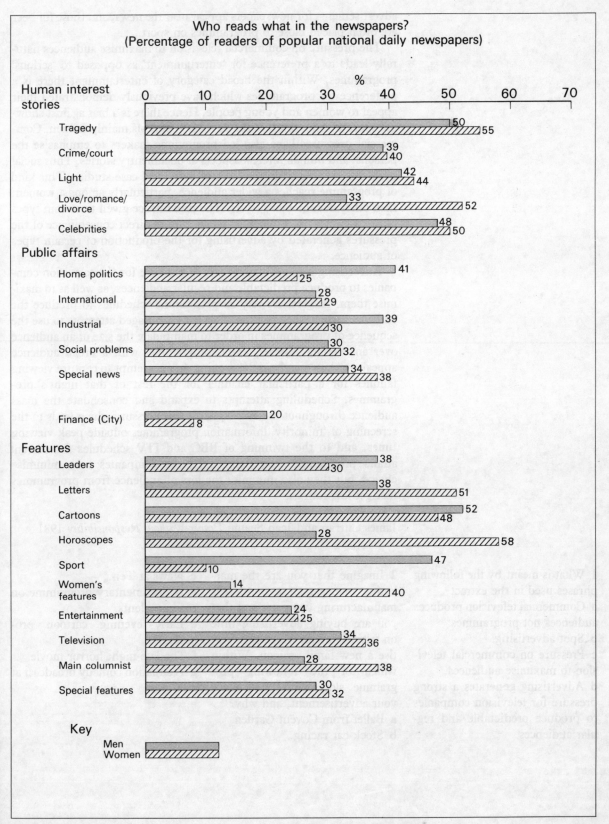

Who reads what in the newspapers?
(Percentage of readers of popular national daily newspapers)

%

Human interest stories

Tragedy — 50 / 55
Crime/court — 39 / 40
Light — 42 / 44
Love/romance/divorce — 33 / 52
Celebrities — 48 / 50

Public affairs

Home politics — 41 / 25
International — 28 / 29
Industrial — 39 / 30
Social problems — 30 / 32
Special news — 34 / 38
Finance (City) — 20 / 8

Features

Leaders — 38 / 30
Letters — 38 / 51
Cartoons — 52 / 48
Horoscopes — 28 / 58
Sport — 47 / 10
Women's features — 14 / 40
Entertainment — 24 / 25
Television — 34 / 36
Main columnist — 28 / 38
Special features — 30 / 32

Key
Men
Women

advertisements for newspapers appear near the news, and those for beer are often placed close to programmes on sport.

The pressure on commercial television to maximise audiences naturally leads to a preference for 'entertainment' as opposed to 'serious' programmes. Within the broad category of entertainment there is a preference for programmes which have previously demonstrated their appeal to women and young people. Hence there is a bias against showing sport at some times of the day – as it appeals mainly to men. Commercial pressures have also led programme makers to emphasise the personal and human interest aspects of documentry stories. Thus social problems are treated in the form of individual case studies. This kind of programme reaches a wider audience, particularly amongst women, than other documentary styles. The prominence given to certain types of programmes on commercial television is a direct consequence of the pressures generated by advertising for the production of certain types of audience.

Advertising also generates a strong pressure for the television companies to produce predictable and regular audiences, as well as to maximise them. Advertisers rely on programme schedules to produce the audiences which they pay for. This has encouraged attempts to use the sequence of programmes in order to manipulate the size of an audience over an evening. Consequently, programmes with a broad audience appeal are shown early in the evening, in an attempt to capture viewing families for a particular channel for the rest of that night's programmes. Scheduling attempts to expand and consolidate the mass audience throughout the evening. It is this pressure which leads to the screening of 'minority' information programmes outside peak viewing times, and to the twinning of BBC and ITV schedules for current affairs programmes. By doing this, the companies may minimise choice, but they also minimise the loss of audience from programmes that get low ratings.

James Curran and Jean Seaton *Power Without Responsibility* 1981

1 What is meant by the following phrases used in the extract?
a Commercial television produces audiences not programmes.
b Spot advertising.
c Pressure on commercial television to maximise audiences.
d Advertising generates a strong pressure for television companies to produce predictable and regular audiences.

2 Imagine that you are the marketing manager of a motor car manufacturing company and that you are buying advertising time on television with which to advertise a new family saloon. Within which of the following programme slots would you place your advertisement, and why?
a Ballet from Covent Garden.
b Stock-car racing.
c News at Ten.
d A documentary programme on road accidents.
e Early evening cartoon programme.
f The late-night horror movie.
g A situation comedy broadcast at 8.00 p.m.

58

Urban growth and decline

How did the industrial areas of Britain's cities develop? The Community Development Projects worked in five such areas: Canning Town, North Shields, Benwell, Batley and Saltley. Here they describe the way the towns grew, matured and then declined.

In each area, the new industries were set up on land formerly used for agriculture or occupied by older industries. During such boom periods, the pressure on land could be so great that it was more profitable for even a profit-making manufacturing concern to close down its operations and sell out the land to one of the new 'growth' industries. In North Shields, land already occupied by glassworks along the Tyne was sold to shipyards and with it these old but once prosperous industries disappeared. In each area the new industrial occupiers gradually acquired their freeholds and laid the basis for a new pattern of ownership which enabled them to sell up in much the same way a century later.

Housing was the other major development that was to transform the 'green fields' of the five areas with, in some cases, the same investors involved in both industrial and housing development. The west end of Newcastle, for example, was a commuting area until the 1870s, with housing for the professional middle classes. Newcastle's working class were forced to live in the slums and 'rookeries' of the town centre. This unbalanced development is not hard to explain, for those same families who controlled the area's industrial development also owned the land, and the provision of working class housing was the least profitable outlet for their capital. As the industries were established more and more workers were needed to run them. Workers were drawn in from other parts of the country, from earlier communities and other lives. In time these uprooted, disorganised people settled in the new areas, found places to live and came to constitute the new 'communities' required to do the work and create the profits of the new industries.

Workers poured into the 'new' towns in a flood of immigration from agricultural and older declining areas where work was fast disappearing. Many were driven by rural destitution from areas where local agriculture had been undermined by new food imports. In some cases capitalists actually forced 'key' workers to migrate: Joseph Wright brought 600 with him to his new carriage works in Saltley, and in Canning Town the descendants of the Scottish workers brought by Lyle from Greenock to produce sugar still live in the streets beside his refinery. In every area there were Irish workers, fleeing the famine.

By the end of the nineteenth century some of the five areas were already at the height of their fortunes as industrial centres. Many local firms were still very profitable and continued to expand. Most of the available industrial land had been occupied during the period of growth, and the remaining sites were now taken over as existing firms expanded or new industry squeezed in.

As the major local industries achieved the peak of their success, this brought with it a kind of stability for the working class communities in most of these places. Even this relative stability of employment and skills was disturbed by sporadic recession, and life remained tough and insecure for most people, with poor incomes, long working hours and hard conditions.

These communities were still growing. In some areas, like Batley, the rate of population increase was much slower than in the early years of growth, and arose less from migration than natural increase. In Canning Town, the population grew as fast as ever up to the First World War. However, in certain parts of each area, the communities were by now well established, and people were able to settle down and organise a new social and political life.

The industrial decline of each area started for different reasons and at different times, and has proceeded at varying speed. The first sign of stagnation and decline were evident in the north east by the turn of the century, while in Saltley the new phase of investment in the motor industry staved off decline until the 1950s.

All five old industrial areas now lie enclosed by more recent industrial and housing development. Beyond Canning Town lie Dagenham and Barking, and the post-war new towns of Basildon and Harlow. On Tyneside, Benwell and North Shields are overshadowed by inter-war estates like Team Valley, and beyond them, the new towns of Cramlington and Washington. But the process that spells decline for the local areas is not a simple one of capital withdrawal. Sometimes it is the very process of investing in new and more productive techniques that is responsible for the loss of many jobs; even increased profitability for industry can mean economic decline for a local community. Furthermore, where major traditional employers have reduced their local operations or even closed down altogether, this is not the end of the story. The decline of the traditional industries has been the signal for new capital to move into these areas, and these new economic activities have rarely provided equivalent new jobs to replace those lost from the older industries. Increasingly, the old working class communities are coming to depend upon a low wage economic structure.

Decline is not a simple process, but one which has many complicating factors and many different stages. The decline of the traditional industries is only the start.

Community Development Projects *The Costs of Industrial Change* 1977

1 List the main features of the growth, maturity and decline in the five areas.

2 How did the changes in local industry affect the lives of the local communities during each period?

3 Explain how the communities lost out both when industry declined *and* when it expanded.

59
Social networks

Family and Kinship in East London by Michael Young and Peter Willmott became a sociological bestseller. It described a way of life in the working class community of Bethnal Green in East London which was soon to disappear. The narrow streets of terraced houses with their corner shops and friendly pubs were soon to be replaced by tower blocks and supermarkets.

The network of social contacts which centred on the family was an important feature of life in established working class communities.

Since family life is so embracing in Bethnal Green, one might perhaps expect it would be all-embracing. The attachment to relatives would then be at the expense of attachment to others. But in practice this is not what seems to happen. Far from the family excluding ties to outsiders, it acts as an important means of promoting them. When a person has relatives in the borough, as most people do, each of these relatives is a go-between with other people in the district. His brother's friends are his acquaintances, if not his friends; his grandmother's neighbours so well known as almost to be his own. The kindred are, if we understand their function aright a bridge between the individual and the community.

The function of the kindred can be understood only when it is realised that long-standing residence is the usual thing. Fifty-three per cent of the people in the general sample were born in Bethnal Green, and over half those born locally had lived in the borough for more than fifteen years. Most people have therefore had time to get to know plenty of other local inhabitants. They share the same background. The people they see when they go out for a walk are people they played with as children. 'I've always known Frank and Barney,' said Mr Sykes. 'We was kids together. We knew each other from so high. We were all in the same street.' They are the people they went to school with. 'It's friendly here,' according to Mrs Warner. 'You can't hardly ever go out without meeting someone you know. Often it's someone you were at school with.' They are the people they knew at the youth club, fellow members of a teenage gang, or boxing opponents. They have the associations of a lifetime in common. If they are brought up from childhood with someone, they may not necessarily like him, they certainly 'know' him. If they live in the same street for long they cannot help getting to know people whom they see every day, talk to and hear about in endless conversation. Long residence by itself does something to create a sense of community with other people in the district. Even an unmarried orphan would have local acquaintances if he were established in this way. But, unmarried orphans being rare, as a rule a person has relatives also living in the district, and as a result his own range of contacts is greatly enlarged. His relatives are also established. Their playmates and their schoolfriends, their workmates and their pub-companions, are people whom he knows as well. Likewise, his friends and acquaintances also have their families in the district, so that when he gets to know any individual person, he is also likely to know at least some of his relatives.

The Bethnal Greener is therefore surrounded not only by his own relatives and their acquaintances, but also by his own acquaintances and their relatives.

Michael Young and Peter Willmott *Family and Kinship in East London* 1960

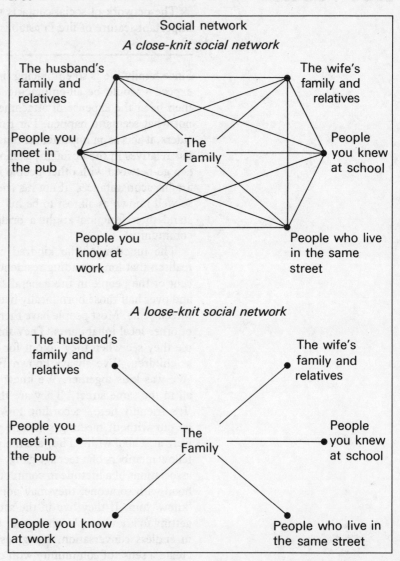

Social network

A close-knit social network

The husband's family and relatives

The wife's family and relatives

People you meet in the pub

The Family

People you knew at school

People you know at work

People who live in the same street

A loose-knit social network

The husband's family and relatives

The wife's family and relatives

People you meet in the pub

The Family

People you knew at school

People you know at work

People who live in the same street

1 What do Young and Willmott mean when they describe the family as 'a bridge between the individual and the community'?

2 Sociologists have used the term 'social networks' to describe the pattern of relationships within a community. Social networks can be either loose-knit or close-knit. We can see the differences between them in the diagram. What kind of social network is described by Young and Willmott in this extract?

3 Shortly after they completed this study Bethnal Green was redeveloped. Modern estates replaced the old streets. It was also a time of greater social mobility with families moving out to the suburbs (see page 141). How would these changes have influenced the established social networks?

60

Woodford and Bethnal Green

Peter Willmott and Michael Young followed their study of family and kinship in East London with a study of Woodford, a London suburb to which many of the people of Bethnal Green had moved.

When we first visited Woodford it was clear that we had come to a different kind of place from Bethnal Green. East End children do not trot their ponies along forest paths wearing velvet hunting caps. East End houses do not have stone gnomes in their backyards. There are no golf courses near the docks.

How few people there seemed to be in Woodford, and how many dogs! This was perhaps what Orwell was talking about when he wrote of 'the huge peaceful wilderness of outer London . . . sleeping the deep, deep sleep of England'. In Bethnal Green there are noisy people everywhere, large mothers with oilskin shopping bags, young mothers in red high-heeled shoes, children playing around the stalls of the street markets, neighbours talking to each other from one door to another. The suburb is sliced by main roads, and the cars and long distance buses speeding to Southend and Newmarket leave only a distant hum in hundreds of empty side roads. In Bethnal Green people are vigorously at home in the streets, their public face much the same as their private. In Woodford people seem to be quieter and more reserved in public.

In Bethnal Green homes and factories are packed tight and surrounded with asphalt, whereas in Woodford the houses are spaced out at intervals and surrounded by grass. 'Traditionally, Woodford has always endeavoured,' says the official guidebook, 'to keep the disadvantages of civilisation at a proper distance without permitting the advantages to escape it.' The disadvantage of civilisation is evidently industry, while the advantages are the cultivated trees and flowers, the garages and the Tudor half-timbering which a modern economy makes possible. The most important physical differences is that there is relatively much more space – in 1959 Woodford had 61,000 people upon 3842 acres, a density of 16 per acre, while Bethnal Green's 49,000 people were pressed in on 760 acres, at a density of 64 to each acre.

The contrast is all the more striking because Woodford and Bethnal Green both belong to East London. Although Woodford is officially is Essex, there is no visible boundary between it and London. Buildings stretch almost all the way from Bethnal Green through Leyton and Woodford, and now even farther out to the belt of new council estates.

The move outwards is also a move upwards. When Mr Lloyd said, with understandable pride, that he had come a long way, he was not thinking of miles. An engineering foreman, he is an example of a man, born in Shadwell, who now owns a six-roomed Edwardian house, red brick with white gate, tiled porch and glass-panelled front door, in a quiet leafy road at Wanstead.

'I've come quite a long way,' he told us, 'from being a Shadwell boy earning 5s a week to having my own house out here.' At 28 he had married a girl from Hackney and to begin with they lived in two rooms at Bow. 'The house came up for sale after a couple of years,' he explained, 'and I tried to buy it. But I couldn't afford it. After that, I said to the wife, "I'm going to work hellish hard the next five years. You help me and I promise you you'll have your own house." And I did it. Six years later I paid the deposit on a small house at Leytonstone. We couldn't afford to furnish the whole house at first, so we let off half of it, but it was a footing, a foundation, something I could build on.' By 1936 he had enough money to pay the deposit on his present house. 'It's a good feeling,' he said, 'the feeling that you've achieved something. Something you've done. Something you're proud of. I could have stayed in the East End, but it didn't appeal to me. I wanted something better for my family. There's always something better than what you've got if only you're prepared to work for it.'

If social class has an edge in Woodford, it is partly because so many of its people come from the East End. 'We don't tell people we come from Bethnal Green,' said one woman, 'You get the scum of the earth there.' Mr Barber said, 'The East End is a different class altogether – people there call you Dad or Uncle or Auntie. We don't get any of that here.'

Although people talk about travelling 'up to town', in this social context 'out' means 'up', up the 'ladder', up 'in the social scale', up 'in the world'. It was as though, in the mind's eye, people had turned the whole of East London on its side like a geological exhibit in a giant-sized museum. There deep down in the lowest strata were Bethnal Green and Stepney and there at the top Woodford and Wanstead. To clamber up the slope was success, to remain at the bottom, failure. Once you had clambered up you wanted to be distinguished as clearly as possible from those who had given up or never tried. This was one reason why people wanted a change in the postal address. Half of the borough was in the same London postal district as the East End. The demand was that the whole should henceforth be known as Essex instead. 'We're under Essex for cricket – when there's a match in Woodford it's the Essex county team – so why shouldn't we be for the post office?'

Peter Willmott and Michael Young *Family and Class in a London Suburb* 1960

1 Make a list of the differences between Woodford and Bethnal Green under each of the following headings:
a the urban environment
b social life
c population density
d recreation and leisure

e social status
f employment.

2 Explain what Mr Lloyd meant when he said he had 'come a long way'. Why was he not thinking of miles?

3 Social class and social status can often be seen in the differences between residential districts. Make a study of two or more districts in your area using the headings above as a basis.

61
No fixed address

In the nineteenth century men like Henry Mayhew, Charles Booth and General William Booth, founder of the Salvation Army, collected evidence on the lives of the poorest people living in the cities. Jonathan Raban's view of the city is very different from the close communities described by Young and Willmott (pages 139–140).

It is as easy to lose other people in a city as it is to mislay one's umbrella. They are always being carried away with the crowd. When the Victorians looked at London, they saw with some shock that one of its chief evils was the ease with which the individual disappeared on the streets. The work of both local government and social and charitable agencies was made harder by the labyrinthine nature of the metropolis. Here was a place where the thief and the footpad could fade into thin air, where those people most in need of help – the poor, the witless, and the diseased – could render themselves invisible in their trek through successions of furnished rooms, where no one could keep track of the citizens who strayed from the narrow path of a permanent home and a permanent job. The image of the nomad, employed independently by Mayhew and by Charles and General William Booth, haunts nineteenth century writing about the city; and nomadism – the vision of a city of aimless and irresponsible wanderers – was seen as just as great a threat to the health of society at large as revolution, destitution and physical disease.

The street-folk whom Mayhew talked to revealed a great deal about the haphazardness of the honeycomb of mid nineteenth century London; a structure into which a person might drop, only to fall and fall, going ever further out of touch with his family and friends. There is no trace now of Mayhew's original questionnaire, but it is clear from the portraits in *London Labour and the London Poor* that he started each conversation by asking how many relatives each of his informants knew, and how frequently they saw them. The answers added up to a general picture of families that were shrinking drastically in size as the husbands or the children went deeper into the city. The closest relatives of many of Mayhew's interviewees had already faded into the distance; and the city immigrant – probably illiterate, certainly inadequately equipped with the basic skills needed to trace and communicate with his family across that widened space which the metropolis brought with it – became a nomad, a loner, scratching acquaintances off the street or in the ginshop. An Irish girl of 22 who sold apples, told Mayhew: 'I'm an orphan, sir, and there's nobody to care for me but God, glory be to his name! I come to London to join my brother, that had come over and did well, and he sent for me, but when I got here I couldn't find him in it anyhow.'

General Booth, whose *In Darkest England and The Way Out* is a remarkably sensitive and humane study of the nineteenth century city, suggested that the Salvation Army should set up an 'Enquiry Office for Lost People':

Perhaps nothing more vividly suggests the varied forms of brokenhearted misery in the great city than the statement that 18,000 people are lost in it every year, of whom 9000 are never heard of any more, anyway in this world. . .Husbands, sons, daughters and mothers are continually disappearing, and leaving no trace behind.

Some of these people were no doubt embracing the darkness of the city, using its streets as an escape, and holing up in some obscure quarter with an assumed name and a new life. Others must just have fallen through, finding themselves fronted with a terrible dead blankness – because they had lost the bit of paper with a crudely inked address, or it had run in the rain, or they had misheard, or the house had been pulled down. . .no name on the doorbell, no address for forwarding, the mistrustful stare of landlady, or new tenant in braces and shirt open at the neck. Suddenly the city must have changed from a labyrinth with a route to its centre into a hopeless scatter of streets, too many to count or imagine, unsignposted and menacing.

For the Victorian writer, the industrial fog which hung over London for so much of the year was very much more than a chemical inconvenience, or even a romantic visual effect; it was the supreme symbol of the city's capacity to make people disappear inside it.

Clean air acts and smokeless zones have largely succeeded in depriving us of the great nineteenth century symbol for losing people. Our modern means are cleaner, less aesthetic and more brutal. People disappear now behind the smoked-glass rear windows of taxis, or into the tartarously-tiled maws of tube stations. They are taken away. The last we see of them is a raised hand, smudgy over a bobbing crowd of heads, or diminishing in size as the traffic lights turn to green. A few months ago, I lost a friend I'd known for five years when she went into the station at Earl's Court. It was, I think, a typical city departure: a stiff kiss, a shifty sideways glance, then blank – nothing at all but the polyglot faces of strangers. . .Arabs, Italians, milk-fed Americans, Australians glumly hulking duffel bags, and F. nowhere. In smaller places, people have to go on living with their social failures; in London there is an uneasy ease of separation. One is so likely to be left only with a phone number in an old address book, and that answered by a strange voice, curt and suspicious. We continually drop each other back into the fog.

Jonathan Raban *Soft City* 1974

1 How is it that people in cities become isolated and separated from others?

2 What are the consequences of this for individuals and for the community?

3 Would you agree or disagree with the following statements? Explain your answer.

a Jonathan Raban describes a city marked by high levels of social integration and social cohesion.

b Raban's city lacks any real social networks.

c Loneliness can be a major problem in a city.

d The city offers people an opportunity to live their own lives outside of the control of relatives or the community.

62

Dealing with urban deprivation

The Community Development Projects (CDP) were established as an answer to the problems of the poorest areas of the inner city. In Coventry CDP worked in the district of Hillfields. The project very soon discovered that many of the assumptions upon which they were expected to work were wrong.

The original model for the national Community Development Projects was based on a belief that there were in our cities small concentrations of people with special problems which demanded special treatment. The Home Secretary in his 1969 speech in Parliament, when he announced the CDP, defined that category of people like this:

> Although the social services cater reasonably well for the majority they are much less effective for a minority who are caught up in a chain reaction of related social problems. An example of the kind of vicious circle in which this kind of family could be trapped is ill health, financial difficulty, children suffering from deprivation, consequent delinquency, inability of the children to adjust to adult life, unstable marriages, emotional problems, ill health – and the cycle begins again.

So it is clear that he had a precise view of the kind of people towards whom CDP was to be directed.

It is clear that the problems are seen as those of social cripples and lame ducks. They are to be helped to make better use of the welfare state first by closer coordination in the delivery of personal services and second by self-help.

Experience in the first two exploratory years of the project forced us to challenge and reject those initial assumptions. First, it became clear that in spite of its reputation, Hillfields did not have an abnormal share of families with personal social handicaps. The most obvious and blatant problems that people experienced were not internal and pathological but were external. They arose from the very low incomes people were having to live on and the very poor housing and environment in the district. These problems were not peculiar to that neighbourhood; they were the same as the problems which were afflicting large sections of the working class population throughout Coventry. They were more acute in their degree but they were not different in kind.

Second, there was little evidence that the problems people experienced resulted from any obvious deterioration in the patterns or values of community life. When we arrived to start work in Coventry at the beginning of 1970, we found that the planners had identified a grid of twenty-six streets which was to be the target area for CDP. This had been selected on the basis of certain assumptions about social problems. Different agencies had been asked to identify where their heaviest problems lay. Some departments had done this in detail and had plotted their caseloads by marking black dots on a street map of the city. Others were much more cavalier and just drew a circle around the area which they believed to have the worst reputation. The planners brought all this information together on base maps, overlaid with census information, and eventually chose a core of twenty-six streets which they saw to be the black spot of the area.

As it happened, we arrived to find that a change in the redevelopment timetable meant that a large part of this core area was to be demolished within a matter of months. Ironically this gave us the opportunity to stand back and ask a lot more questions about the ways in which the area's reputation as a blackspot had arisen. We came to see that this was less a reflection of deteriorating standards of local community behaviour, than of processes external to the locality. The area's reputation for prostitution is a good illustration. Statistics of court convictions for 'loiter prostitution' would certainly show a heavy preponderance in Hillfields. But levels of surveillance by the vice squad are also greatest in Hillfields. A self-fulfilling prophecy seemed to be at work, whereby the police were more alert to this phenomenon in Hillfields than in other districts and so their levels of detection and hence conviction were also greater. In fact, it seems that the prostitution in the district is almost entirely a commuter business. It is not local women but women from the West Midlands who come from as far away as Nottingham to solicit in Hillfields. Their clients are not Hillfields men either but commuters from other parts of Coventry or the city region. So the 'malaise' statistics record a number of phenomena which have little connection with any deterioration of community values in Hillfields.

The third thing that became clear was that local people did not see more communication leading to better solutions to their problems at all. On the contrary, they were in direct dispute with the authorities about the nature of their needs and their aspirations. They saw the problem as their difficulty in influencing decisions which affected their lives in the directions which they wanted. It was a situation where residents believed they had a different interest from that represented by the public authorities. Communication was there in plenty; communication that was only sometimes vocal or articulate, expressed mostly in informal social settings, but sometimes through the traditional means of petitions and public meetings and at times of exceptional frustration, even in minor acts of insurrection. One local resident was prepared to barricade himself in his house and put live electric cables around to keep the bulldozers at bay. That seemed to be a fairly clear message.

So it became clear to us that the initial prescriptions of CDP were inadequate to the actual situation. The diagnosis was incorrect. The solution for Hillfields could not be looked for in stronger doses of the medicine that the welfare state had been serving up, or in a better mixing of ingredients in that dose, or even in a better bedside manner in the administering of the dose. We were in fact confronted by problems of politics, the problem of conflicts of interests in the city, and the problem of powerlessness in influencing political decisions.

John Bennington *The Flaw in the Pluralist Heaven* 1975

I KNOW I LEFT MY FLAT AROUND HERE SOMEWHERE!

1 What do you understand by the following terms used in the passage?

a social cripples
b pathological
c case loads
d black spots
e redevelopment
f self-fulfilling prophecy
g diagnosis
h prescription

2 Why were CDP set up in the first place?

3 What kind of problems were they supposed to deal with? How were they intended to deal with them?

4 Why did the project reject the earlier assumptions? What were the real problems faced by Hill-fields?

5 In what ways might the town planners, social workers and the police have added to Hillfields' problems and its poor reputation?

6 John Bennington makes a comparison with a doctor's methods when he writes that the diagnosis was wrong and therefore the wrong medicine was prescribed. On the basis of the revised diagnosis made by CDP what 'medicine' do you think would help to solve some of the problems of Hillfields?

63

Religious behaviour

Going to church or to Sunday school, reading the Bible or saying your prayers are activities which we would describe as religious. By measuring changes in this type of behaviour sociologists attempt to gain a picture of how religion is changing. Michael Argyle and Benjamin Beit-Hallami consider some of the evidence.

Church attendance has been studied in a number of local surveys, and more recently by reported church attendance in social surveys. The local surveys are more accurate, but there are wide variations from one area to another, and it is difficult to draw general conclusions from them. There are also difficulties about the proportion of people who go twice on Sundays. Social surveys cover larger areas, but are subject to quite large sampling errors, and there are discrepancies between different surveys in the same year.

Since there were no social surveys at the turn of the century, we must depend on counts of attendance in particular areas. Counts in 25 English cities found an average Sunday attendance of 38 per cent of the population in 1881 (Chadwick, 1966). Correction for those who went twice, estimated at 40 per cent, reduces this to 27 per cent. Later counts in other cities, corrected in a similar way, show that about 25 per cent of the adult population attended in Liverpool in 1902 (Jones, 1934) and 25 per cent in York in 1901 (Rowntree and Lavers, 1951).

The level of church attendance in recent years can be obtained from social surveys, though the percentages obtained vary with the area covered and the time of year. A good survey of people in Britain aged over 21 was conducted for *New Society* by the National Opinion Poll in 1965, and was reported by Goldman. This showed that 16.9 per cent of the sample had been to church in the previous week. Other surveys found 14–15 per cent attendance. There appears to have been a decline of weekly church attendance from 25 per cent for England in 1900 to about 15 per cent in 1965.

Table 10 Church attendance in Britain in 1900 and 1965–70 (as a percentage of the population)

1900	1900 for one Sunday	previous week	1965–70 previous 3 months*
Church of England	10	5	24.1
Nonconformists (inc. Church of Scotland)	11	4	9.4
Roman Catholics	3	5	6.7
Jews	–	0.2	0.8
Other religions	–	0.8	1.5

(From various sources. *From Goldman, 1965.)

This decline has varied between denominations. Part of the decline in church attendance is due to a change in the frequency with which individuals go to church. The proportion of those who went twice on a Sunday fell from about 40 per cent in 1909 to 8 per cent in 1947, and is now probably lower still, following the decline of evening service. The Church of England has a large proportion of members who go less than once a week. In addition, 68 per cent of the population of England and Wales are married in church, 80 per cent are baptised, and 67 per cent claim to belong to it.

Radio and television provide another way of attending services. On any Sunday about 24 per cent of the adult population watch BBC religious programmes, and 18 per cent see ITV programmes; as many as 45 per cent make a point of watching or listening to broadcast services. The most popular programme was 'Songs of Praise', watched by 35 per cent of the population. Of course the level of attention may not be very high, since some people simply leave their sets switched on, more or less permanently.

There has been a big decline in Sunday school membership since 1900. At that time 30 per cent of children belonged to Church of England Sunday schools alone. This has dropped to 13 per cent by 1960. Nonconformist Sunday school membership has fallen in a similar way. On the other hand, family services have become more common. Sixty-nine per cent of parents still wanted Christian religious education in schools in 1965.

About 44 per cent of the adult population claim to pray every day, mostly before going to bed. This rather high percentage is supported by a number of other surveys. What they pray about are family and friends, especially for those who are ill, happier family life, peace, and help for self in crises. An even larger number, about 58 per cent, teach their children to pray. Bible reading is much less common: about 11 per cent read it regularly at home, nonconformists more than others. About 22 per cent belong to church groups, 33 per cent for nonconformists.

Michael Argyle and Benjamin Beit-Hallami *The Social Psychology of Religion* 1975

1 How has church attendance changed since 1900? Have the changes affected all churches in the same way?

2 What has caused these changes?

3 Is it true to say that a fall in church attendance indicates a decline in religious belief? Give reasons for your answer.

4 How has the pattern of family worship changed?

5 Using the most recent evidence what percentage of the adult or child population:
a pray every day?
b have attended church in the previous week?

c listen to religious programmes on the radio?
d have been baptised into the Church of England?
e read the Bible regularly?
f watch religious programmes on the television?
g belong to church groups?
h have been married in church?

64

Family religion

Eva Sjoqvist was brought up on the Swedish island of Aggarö. Religion played an important part in the life of the island community.

Both Mom and Dad were nonconformists and members of the Pentecostal Church. Grandmother was a Baptist, and grandfather became one in later years. Earlier generations of our family have also been nonconformist.

We weren't able to go to the meetings very often from Aggarö, but Dad used to have family services at home on Sundays. On the second day of Christmas we went to the Sunday school party in Västerås, the whole bunch of us. We rode with Mr Hålldin, and it was the only day during the entire year that we took a taxi. Mom usually had a lot of trouble getting all the boys neatly dressed.

Somebody read a passage from the Bible, then people sang and acted out little plays, and there were games and packages of goodies. About three hundred kids from the Pentecostal Sunday schools in the neighbourhood of Västerås took part. Sunday school didn't start in Kärrbo until I was a bit older, so I never went to one.

I can't remember us kids ever being teased during our school years because we were religious. Everyone knew us for what we were. We didn't make a big thing out of it either – we were really no different from anybody else.

The evangelists used to like to visit us and we would hold meetings sometimes in the kitchen. Folks from Aggarö and even from Harkie came to these meetings. In winter we occasionally rode over the ice by sled to Ridö and went to the meetings at Hugo Andersson's house. He was the man who regained his sight after an operation in 1968, after having been almost blind for thirty-six years.

Most often the Kärrbo group's prayer meetings were held in Karelen. I think the cottage there was owned by the workers' community in Irsta, and they would rent it each time. The congregation in Västerås employed two evangelists who lived in the Elim Chapel in Kungsåra, and who were sent around to help the local members with their meetings. The local members would speak up or sing, according to their ability. Once a month members came out from Västerås to 'the outposts', and there was usually singing and music. Between times, assembly days were held for the members in the neighbourhood.

My brothers and sister weren't confirmed. We went to the Pentecostal Church but were not members; you're counted as a member from the time of baptism, which doesn't take place at any special time, but only when you yourself decide. Some children were baptised when they were eight or nine years old. I was baptised in 1938, when I was fourteen.

I had made up my own mind then. Faith probably comes through preaching, actually, and I had heard a lot of sermons. Naturally your environment plays a role too. Mom and Dad wanted us children to follow in their footsteps. Most of the young people we went around with were believers too. I still belong to the congregation. You feel secure having a foundation to stand on.

At baptisms several people are usually baptised at the same time. First of all you have to make a confession in front of the congregation at a meeting; you tell how you were saved and when you really began being a believer.

Some were a little shy but generally believers are less shy than other people, since they want to do something to spread the faith, or at least try. It makes it easier too that there's a sympathetic atmosphere when the youngsters make their confession.

I was baptised along with three or four others. We wore white baptismal robes which reached down to our feet and white stockings, but no shoes. The robe had weights on the hem to prevent it from floating up during the ceremony.

We stood together in order of height, and then the minister who was to perform the baptism read from the Bible about baptism and its significance. One at a time we stepped down into the baptismal pool.

The congregation sings one verse of a song after which the act of baptism takes place, when the minister says the name of the person to be baptised and reads the baptism ritual. Then the one being baptised is immersed under the water and at that point the old person is buried. At the same time the congregation sings verse two of the hymn.

Afterwards we went out through a side door and got dressed again, and then the members of the congregation welcomed us and talked to us, saying how joyful they were that we'd been baptised. I had promised to live a Christian life and to me it was a great day. I received my membership card some time later.

Sture Källberg *Report from a Swedish Village* 1972

1 Describe how Eva Sjoqvist became a member of the church? Was her baptism different from any baptisms you have attended?

2 In Eva's family, religion was not just a matter of going to church on Sunday. Explain why.

3 Most religious groups have certain members who hold positions of authority and may even be paid employees of the church. Use a dictionary to find out what the following religious leaders do:
a evangelist
b priest
c bishop
d deacon
e minister
f missionary
g vicar
h elder.
Some of these terms have more than one meaning and you may have to choose the definition which is most appropriate.

65

Religious belief

Who believes what in British society? Surveys on beliefs have been carried out regularly during the past 30 years. What do they tell us about the way beliefs change and about religion in Britain

A Gallup poll into religious beliefs in Britain, conducted for *The Sunday Telegraph*, shows that belief in Christ as the Son of God and in the divine authority of the Bible is falling among the British public, but belief in God and Heaven shows some increase.

Between March 21 and 26, Gallup asked a nationally representative sample of 918 adults: 'which, if any, of the following do you believe in?' and the replies were:

Table 11

	Today	1975	1973	1968
God	76	72	74	77
Heaven	57	49	51	54
Reincarnation	28	22	22	18
The Devil	22	20	18	21
Hell	22	20	20	23

As the following analysis shows, women more than men and the not-so-young more than the young believe in God and Heaven; while belief in reincarnation, the Devil and Hell is more evenly spread:

*"But don't you see? If I answered your prayer, I'd have to answer **everybody's** prayer."*

Table 12

	God	Heaven	Reincarnation	Devil	Hell
Overall	76	57	28	22	22
Men	68	47	23	20	20
Women	83	66	33	24	24
16–24	62	45	28	25	20
25–34	68	45	33	24	21
35–44	78	60	26	21	25
45–64	82	62	26	19	21
65+	86	70	30	23	24

Analysis by frequency of church going shows similar sharp differences, and also shows that non-attendance at church does not necessarily mean a lack of religious beliefs.

For example, while 96 per cent of those claiming to go to church at least once a month believe in God, 52 per cent of those who never, or almost never, go also believe in God. Belief in Heaven drops from 78 per cent to 39 per cent respectively, between these two groups.

Belief in a personal god has fallen slightly and belief in some sort of spirit or life force has risen, as measured by replies to the questions: 'Which of these statements comes closest to your belief?'

Table 13

	Today	1963	1957
There is a personal god	33	38	41
There is some sort of spirit, a life force	41	33	37
I don't know what to think	16	20	16
I don't really think there is any sort of spirit or life force	8	9	6

Again, men and young adults are less likely to believe in a personal god than are women and the elderly. While 25 per cent of men believe in a personal god and 44 per cent think there is some sort of spirit or life force, the figures for women are 43 per cent and 40 per cent respectively.

Fewer people now think that Jesus Christ was the Son of God, though this belief is still held by the majority of the general public.

Replies to the question: 'Do you believe that Jesus Christ was the Son of God or just a man?' were:

Table 14

	Today	1963	1957
Son of God	55	60	71
Just a man	25	16	9
Just a story	7	7	6
Don't know	13	17	14

Belief in Christ as the Son of God is highest among those claiming to go to church at least once a month (88 per cent), women (65 per cent) and those aged 65 and over (61 per cent).

Eighty per cent of those claiming to go to church at least once a month think that the Bible is essential to the Christian Church, compared with only 49 per cent of those who never, or almost never, go to church.

Sunday Telegraph 1979

1 What is the source of the evidence in the article?

2 Seventy-six per cent of all of those interviewed in this 1979 survey believed in God. In which of the following groups is there a higher proportion of believers, and in which is there a lower proportion?
a men
b people over 65 years old
c people interviewed in 1975
d people under 25 years old
e women
f people interviewed in 1968.

3 What trend is there in people's belief in:
a God;
b reincarnation;
c the Devil?

What conclusions might you draw from these figures? Why might you view evidence such as this with caution?

4 Why is it difficult to make a link between people's claimed beliefs and attendance at church?

5 How have people's views about Jesus Christ changed since 1957?

Subject index

Author Index

ARGYLE, M. and BEIT-HALLAMI, B. *The Social Psychology of Religion*, Routledge and Kegan Paul 1975.

BARNES, D. *From Communication to Curriculum*, Penguin 1976.

BELLABY, P. *The Sociology of Comprehensive Schooling*, Methuen 1977.

BENNINGTON, J. *The Flaw in the Pluralist Heaven*, from: Lees, R. and Smith, G. *Action Research and Community Development*, Routledge and Kegan Paul 1975.

BLISHEN, E. *The School that I'd Like*, Penguin 1969.

BRAVERMAN, H. *Labour and Monopoly Capital*, Monthly Review Press 1974.

COMMUNITY DEVELOPMENT PROJECTS *The Costs of Industrial Change*, CDP Inter-Project Team 1977.

CURRAN, J. and SEATON, J. *Power without Responsibility*, Fontana 1981.

DAVIE, R., BUTLER, N. and GOLDSTEIN, H. *From Birth to Seven*, Longman 1972.

DITTON, J. *Monotony at Work*, New Society 21 December 1972.

DITTON, J. *Part-time Crime*, Macmillan 1977.

DUMMETT, A. *A Portrait of English Racism*, Penguin 1973.

EDWARDS, R. *The trials of Miss Snobby Snout*, New Statesman 7 November 1980.

FAULDER, C. *Women's Magazines*, from: King, J. and Stott, M. *Is this your life? Images of women in the media*, Virago/Quartet 1977.

GARVEY, A. *Women in Pubs*, New Society 21 February 1974

GIBSON, T. *People Power*, Penguin 1979.

GLASGOW MEDIA GROUP *Bad News* Volume 1, Routledge and Kegan Paul 1976.

HADDON, R. *The Location of West Indians in the London Housing Market*, from: *New Atlantis* Volume 2 1970.

HANSON, D. and HERRINGTON, M. *'Please Miss you're supposed to stop her'*, Society Today No. 24 1 June 1978.

HARKER, D. *One for the Money*, Hutchinson 1980.

HEATH, A. *Social Mobility*, Fontana 1981.

KÄLLBERG, S. *Report from a Swedish Village*, Penguin 1972.

KELLNER, P. *When the window shopping has to stop*, New Statesman 27 November 1981.

KETTLE, M. *The Mystery of the Radical Young*, New Society 12 April 1979.

KING, A. *A Sociological Portrait: Politics*, from Barker, P. *A Sociological Portrait*, Penguin 1972.

LAYE, C. *The African Child*, Fontana 1969.

LOFTUS, H. *Beware the County Crackdown*, Drive Magazine 1974.

MCINTOSH, M. *Changes in the Organisation of Thieving*, from: Cohen, S. *Images of Deviance*, Penguin 1971.

MACK, J. *Schools for Privilege*, New Society 7 July 1977.

MARSH, P. *Life and careers on the football terraces*, from Ingham, R. *Football Hooliganism*, Inter-Action Trust 1978.

MARSHALL, J.V. *Walkabout*, Michael Joseph 1959.

MARX, K. and ENGELS, F. *The Communist Manifesto*, from: Feuer, L.S. *Marx and Engels Basic Writings*, Collins 1959.

MEAD, M. *Coming of Age in Samoa*, Penguin 1943.

MILLS, C.W. *The Sociological Imagination*, Penguin 1970.

MITCHELL, G.D. *A Dictionary of Sociology*, Routledge 1968.

NEWMAN, B. *Holidays and Social Class*, from: Smith, M.A. et al *Leisure and Society in Britian*, Allen Lane 1973.

NICOLAUS, M. *Sociology Liberation Movement*, from: Pateman, T. *Counter Course*, Penguin 1972.

OAKLEY, A. *The Sociology of Housework*, Martin Robertson 1974.

ORWELL, G. *Shooting an Elephant*, from: *Inside the Whale and other essays*, Penguin 1957.

PATRICK, J. *A Glasgow Gang Observed*, Eyre Methuen 1973.

PERRY, T. and BOYD, M. *Roman Nights, Society Today* 20   17 February 1978.

RABAN, J. *Soft City*, Hamish Hamilton 1974.

RICHMAN, J. *Busmen versus the public*, *New Society* 14 August 1969.

ROBERTS, R. *The Classic Slum*, Penguin 1971.

ROWBOTHAM, S. *Woman's Consciousness, Man's World*, Penguin 1973.

SEDGEMORE, B. *The Secret Constitution*, Hodder and Stoughton 1980.

SHARPE, S. *Just Like a Girl*, Penguin 1976.

SHILS, E. and YOUNG, M. *The meaning of the Coronation*, *Sociological Review* Volume 1 1953.

SILVERMAN, D. *An Analysis of Traditional Sociology*, from Filmer, D. et al *New Directions in Sociological Theory*, Collier-Macmillan 1972.

SMITH, D.J. *The Facts of Racial Disadvantage*, PEP 1976.

STACY, M., BATSTONE, E., BELL, C., and MURCOTT, A. *Power, Persistence and Change: a second study of Banbury*, Routledge and Kegan Paul 1975.

TOYNBEE, P. *A Working Life*, Hodder and Stoughton 1971.

TUNSTALL, J. *The Fishermen*, McGibbon and Kee 1962.

TUNSTALL, J. *Journalists at Work*, Constable 1971.

TYLER, W., *The Sociology of Educational Inequality*, Methuen 1977.

WATSON, J. *Between Two Cultures*, Blackwell 1977.

WEDDERBURN, D. *Divisions in the Work Place*, *New Society* 9 April 1970.

WEIGHTMAN, G. *The Tricky Game of Population Trends*, *New Society* 16 February 1978

WILLIS, P. *Lads, Lobes and Labour*, *New Society* 27 November 1976.

WILLMOTT, P. and YOUNG, M. *Family and Class in a London Suburb*, Routledge and Kegan Paul 1960.

WILSON, D. *So you want to be a Prime Minister*, Penguin 1979.

WISER, W. and WISER, C. *Behind Mud Walls*, University of California Press 1963.

YOUNG, M. and WILLMOTT, P. *Family and Kinship in East London*, Routledge and Kegan Paul 1960.

YOUNG, M. and WILLMOTT, P. *The Symmetrical Family*, Penguin 1975.

Illustration acknowledgements

We are grateful to the following for permission to reproduce cartoons:

Rupert Besley, page 56; Michael ffolkes, page 22; Ian Kellas, page 18; London Express News and Feature Services, pages 84 (Giles, Daily Express), 104 and 106 (JAK, Evening Standard); Edward McLachlan, page 17 and cover; John Minnion, page 131; New Yorker, page 82; A.D. Peters and Co Ltd (Posy Simmonds) page 43; Punch, pages 12 (Graham), 28 (Larry), 33 (Anthony), 66 (Hector Breeze), 93 (Edward McLachlan) 119 and 152 (A.J. Spoop); Syndication International, Mirror Group Newspapers, pages 89 and 115.

For information concerning artwork we are grateful to:

P. Bellamy, *The Sociology of Comprehensive Schooling*, Methuen, page 53; J. Curran and J. Seaton, *Power Without Responsibility*, Fontana, page 135; Institute of British Geographers, page 75; K.K. Sillitoe, *Planning for Leisure*, 1969, page 81 and *Social Trends*, pages 97, 120 and 122, reproduced with permission from Her Majesty's Stationery Office; David Turner, The Guardian, page 47; G. Weightman, *The Tricky Game of Population Trends*, New Society, page 26.